T0311720

Systemic Thinking for Public Managers

Offering a pathway to vibrant organizations, this book integrates systems thinking, critical thinking, and design thinking and provides the tools needed to apply them proactively in the social systems where we live and work.

Systemic thinking—the combination of systems thinking, critical thinking, and design thinking—provides a way of addressing the complexity of problems faced by public sector managers. Far too often, systemic thinking has been discussed theoretically rather than practically. This book changes that, enabling public sector managers and leaders to connect staff, partners, and stakeholders in the pursuit of thoughtfully designed and responsive service. Clearly written and designed to be put to immediate use on the job, each chapter provides a discussion of a specific practice. Included are guiding principles, a case study, relevant practical tools, and suggestions for additional practice and reading.

Using this book, managers of social systems such as child welfare, healthcare, public schools and libraries, housing and community development, and students of public administration will gain a deeper understanding of organizational systems and design and a new toolkit to fortify their own organizations.

Sheila E. Murphy, PhD, has served as a consultant to government, private sector, and nonprofit organizations for 30 years. She served on the faculty of the School of Public Affairs at Arizona State University, where she co-designed and instructed the 10-month Certified Public Manager program, serving federal, tribal, state, county, and municipal government professionals.

Tracey A. Regenold, PhD, works as a public sector management consultant. Her previous experience includes working in nonprofit organizations providing direct service to adults from vulnerable populations and designing instruction for public manager education. Tracey earned her doctoral degree in workforce education from Old Dominion University. She holds a Master of Public Administration from Arizona State University.

Philip A. Reed, PhD, DTE, is a professor in the Darden College of Education and Professional Studies at Old Dominion University in Norfolk, Virginia. He has served as a teacher, teacher educator, and administrator in secondary and post-secondary education for over 30 years. His research focuses on curriculum development and implementation in workforce education.

Systemic Thinking for Public Managers

Five Practices for Creating a Vibrant Organization

Sheila E. Murphy,
Tracey A. Regenold,
and Philip A. Reed

Routledge
Taylor & Francis Group

NEW YORK AND LONDON

Designed cover image: Dawn Larder

First published 2024
by Routledge
605 Third Avenue, New York, NY 10158

and by Routledge
4 Park Square, Milton Park, Abingdon, Oxon, OX14 4RN

Routledge is an imprint of the Taylor & Francis Group, an informa business

© 2024 Sheila E. Murphy, Tracey A. Regenold, and Philip A. Reed

The right of Sheila E. Murphy, Tracey A. Regenold, and Philip A. Reed to be identified as authors of this work has been asserted in accordance with sections 77 and 78 of the Copyright, Designs and Patents Act 1988.

Library of Congress Cataloging-in-Publication Data
Names: Murphy, Sheila, Ph. D., author. | Regenold, Tracey A., author. | Reed, Philip A., author.
Title: Systemic thinking for public managers : five practices for creating a vibrant organization / Sheila Murphy, Tracey A. Regenold and Philip A. Reed.
Description: New York, NY : Routledge, 2024.
Identifiers: LCCN 2023052374 (print) | LCCN 2023052375 (ebook) | ISBN 9781032370712 (hardback) | ISBN 9781032370668 (paperback) | ISBN 9781003335153 (ebook)
Subjects: LCSH: Industrial management. | Critical thinking. | System theory. | Strategic planning.
Classification: LCC HD31 .M827 2024 (print) | LCC HD31 (ebook) | DDC 658—dc23/eng/20231120
LC record available at https://lccn.loc.gov/2023052374
LC ebook record available at https://lccn.loc.gov/2023052375

ISBN: 978-1-032-37071-2 (hbk)
ISBN: 978-1-032-37066-8 (pbk)
ISBN: 978-1-003-33515-3 (ebk)

DOI: 10.4324/9781003335153

Typeset in Sabon
by Apex CoVantage, LLC

This book is dedicated to all those who teach and learn in social systems.

Contents

Preface

The idea for this book evolved over many years of working with public managers in educational programs and in consulting arrangements, observing their work, engaging in dialogue, conducting evaluation research, and conducting action research projects with them. Our idea deepened through dissertation research by one of the authors exploring a systems approach to the public system of workforce development, emphasizing strategic planning, systems design, and visualization. We continued reading research, exploring theories, and examining practices in the areas of management, public administration, organizational development, and education. Our experience, learning, and reflecting about work and practice led us to realize three forms of abstract thinking that intrigued us, showed promise in practice, and seemed worthy of developing: Systems thinking, critical thinking, and design thinking. Together, these three comprise what we refer to as systemic thinking.

After reviewing literature on systems thinking, critical thinking, and design thinking, we conducted action research and design-based research to design systemic thinking tools. The design-based research was conducted with instructional designers and public managers to determine principles for designing and refining systemic thinking tools. Our research yielded a broad array of useful perspectives and suggestions that we used to develop the one-page tools included in this book.

We know that in traditional public management thinking, rational decision-making is promoted. Rational decision-making depends on acquiring, processing, and analyzing all available information. Public managers know all too well that such a requirement does not withstand the pressure test of practice. Busy professionals in public service often need to make difficult decisions rapidly and under pressure—due to such circumstances as budgetary constraints or politics—and often cannot spare the time needed to gather, sort, or make sense of all the information they would need to make a rational decision. This problem of too much information to review and too little time to make decisions is not new; public managers have known and lamented this for decades.

Merely acquiring extensive data does not solve problems. We argue that it is more difficult to manage complexity when relying solely on information and data. Abstract thinking has a vital role to play: It offers a flexible and impactful skill set that can be applied to any situation. The ability to engage in abstract thinking such as systemic thinking becomes a useful asset to foster creative thought and generate new approaches. Just as theory leads to practice, systemic thinking leads to concrete actions that add value to public service. Skilled managers learn to think of concepts abstractly and to put their thinking into action. And when multiple people work together to apply such cognitive skills, complexity becomes more manageable.

Another common refrain the public sector has endured over the years is: Be more like business! Yet businesses are drowning in almost as much information as the public sector and do not face nearly so much complexity as their public sector counterparts. The public sector is a complex arena that requires listening, sensitivity, and a willingness to design new realities that better serve those who need social services.

Some public managers are already trained in forms of abstract thought such as strategic thinking and quantitative thinking. While useful and necessary, such forms of thought are no longer sufficient to meet the needs of today's evolving social systems. Realizing that we wanted to develop practical ways to teach systems thinking, critical thinking, and design thinking, we researched original works on the topics. We examined materials from a social system perspective—to see what would work, what could be applied, and what might be adapted to serve the public sector and its clients. We also wanted to incorporate the philosophy behind these abstract thinking skills.

We recognize the important role our chosen field of education plays in teaching abstract thinking skills. We believe knowledge is a constructive process that must account for prior learning and experience. Adults bring experience, expertise, and professionalism to a learning opportunity that must be respected. When introduced to abstract thinking skills such as systems thinking, critical thinking, and design thinking, context is also relevant. We wanted to contextualize these abstract thinking skills within professional practices with which public managers are already familiar, such as collaboration, culture building, etc., to help simplify and clarify their use.

With this book, we sought to provide a practical guide based on foundational literature and research and shaped in a practical fashion to meet the current and future needs of managers of public sector social systems. In our view, systemic thinking represents a tremendous capability that public managers can use to navigate the complexity inherent in their considerable responsibilities. We hope that public managers will benefit while modeling the practices and approaches we have developed to create vibrant organizations that serve their clients and communities.

We would like to thank the research participants who guided our thinking as we shaped the tools for this book. We acknowledge with gratitude Dawn Larder for the cover art and Tracey A. Regenold and Dawn Larder for the illustrations of the authors' tool designs. We also extend our appreciation to the many public sector professionals with whom we have worked throughout the years who inspired the writing of this book. We also thank Bethany Nelson for her editorial support of the manuscript. We appreciate Old Dominion University for reviewing and approving the research that contributed to this book. We are very appreciative of M. Aaron Bond and Daniel Schwartz, who introduced us to Meredith Norwich at Routledge. This book would not have been possible without those introductions and without Meredith's support of our ideas.

Chapter 1

Introduction

Systemic Thinking

Systemic thinking is a mode of thinking that is holistic, focused on organizations as systems, aware of boundaries, and aware of the communication that occurs between systems (Boardman & Sauser, 2013). Systemic thinking is inclusive of other forms of thought that support understanding and managing a system. In this book, systemic thinking is comprised of systems thinking, critical thinking, and design thinking, as shown in Figure 1.1.

Systems thinking is an inclusive approach to management and leadership that seeks input from diverse perspectives. Critical thinking drives analysis and decision-making through the questioning of assumptions, thus regulating systems thinking. Design thinking occurs during a process of synthesis in which holistic and analytical thinking are brought together to help shift the status quo of an organization to a more vibrant reality. These shifts may occur by creating new policies, processes, or programs or by redesigning existing ones.

Other ways of thinking could be included in systemic thinking, such as creative thinking, egalitarian thinking, strategic thinking, etc., to help support and manage a social system. However, we will focus on systems thinking, critical thinking, and design thinking as the foundations of systemic thinking. It should be noted that systemic thinking is not the same as systematic thinking. Systematic thinking involves taking steps in a linear, orderly process (Swanson & Dobbs, 2006). Systemic thinking may include systematic processes but focuses on making connections (often non-linear) to fulfill organizational purposes. Our intention with this book is to provide clear, accessible material on systemic thinking for public managers in all types of social systems for the benefit of the communities served.

Applying systemic thinking throughout the organization provides a dynamic and holistic way of exploring challenges. Throughout this book, we employ a systemic thinking approach to common organizational

DOI: 10.4324/9781003335153-1

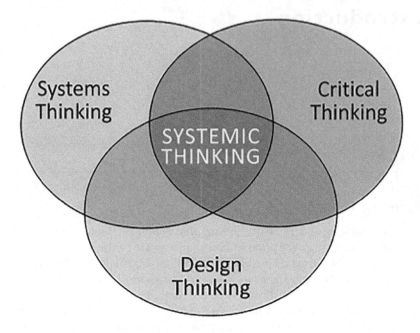

Figure 1.1 Systemic Thinking.

activities such as evaluation, collaboration, and culture development, empowering public managers of social systems to create vibrant organizations. The context of common organizational activities provides a familiar foundation for learning abstract ideas.

Systems Thinking

C. West Churchman (1913–2004) was a systems scholar and professor at the University of California, Berkeley, who taught and influenced many of the prominent systems thinkers from the late 20th century to today. Churchman (1968) described systems thinking as a way of conceptualizing organizational life that promotes everyone's working toward a single, holistic purpose. Thinking of an organization as a system promotes purpose-driven action and supports connections and relationships among people, departments, partner organizations, and multiple environments (e.g., social, political, economic, ecological). Promoting commitment to a shared purpose provides a meaningful foundation for transforming your organization over time.

An organization can be perceived as the entity that brings the parts together to form a system (Churchman, 1971). Organizations are systems comprised of structures, processes, rules, procedures, and roles to carry them out using strategies to fulfill missions and values (Schön, 1983). A social system organization, perceived from a systemic thinking standpoint, is one in which service is the essential vehicle or means to purpose fulfillment (Nelson & Stolterman, 2014).

It is important to note that the primary type of systems thinking we focus on in this book is what is known as soft systems thinking (Checkland, 1999). Soft systems thinking proposes that we go beyond thinking about tangible system structures and pay more attention to making systemic connections in our own minds: Connections that pertain to processes, departments, and people delivering value to the public. While we include the use of other types of systems thinking where appropriate, soft systems thinking is primarily suited for the human interactions prevalent within social systems.

Critical Thinking

Critical thinking is the process of using and assessing logic that supports the establishment of positions, the preparation of arguments, or the making of decisions (Diestler, 2020). One of the most transformative aspects of critical thinking is the ability to identify one's own assumptions: Assumptions about how organizations are structured, how funding streams are deployed, and who should have a seat at the table when decisions are made. Assumptions need to be tested and challenged.

Critical thinking includes understanding and addressing these assumptions (Diestler, 2020), since these assumptions helped establish an organization's culture, rhetoric, and policies. Most important, however, is understanding that the assumptions, rhetoric, and policies underlying an organization's structure and culture have been socially constructed. Social constructions are not truths set in stone, but societal inventions that were introduced at one time, developed over time, have been changed before, and can be changed again.

Design Thinking

Design thinking entails the combining of different elements, such as analytical and holistic thinking, that allow for the creation of a new reality (Buchanan, 1992; Gharajedaghi, 2011; Nelson & Stolterman, 2014). The new reality may occur in the form of a program, policy, service, or process. Design thinking can also emerge from a combination of systems thinking and critical thinking. For example, while identifying an organization's purpose, someone may reflect on who designed the purpose, the assumptions that led to its creation, and what constructs are being sustained by those assumptions. Reflection on these topics may then lead to insights about how to re-design a process, department, or entire system to serve the public more effectively and sustainably. In short, design thinking supports the shifting of ideas from abstract space to concrete matter: In and of itself, it is the space of progress.

Vibrant Organizations

This book is premised on the value of creating a vibrant organization. A vibrant organization is a conscious organization that embraces its systemic reality and continuously produces transformative value for the clients it serves. We assert that public social systems serve as beacons for the community, functioning as vibrant organizations reflective of the best humanity has to offer for the betterment of society. We are also aware that within some spheres of public life, there are social systems that are already vibrant organizations and may be seeking to re-create their vibrancy. There are also social systems that have the potential to be created and managed as vibrant organizations, thriving in and contributing to the community.

Social Systems and Their Public Managers

Social systems often serve vulnerable populations, such as people experiencing poverty or homelessness, those experiencing mental illness, or people who have experienced justice system involvement. These social systems educate, employ, feed, or house people of all ages. In other words, social systems serve humanity.

Public managers of social systems may work in a government agency, in a nonprofit or third-sector organization, in a non-governmental organization, or in a public school at any level. As a public manager, you may be someone who wants to make a difference in a department, organization, community, or in the world. You may also be interested in affecting your organization's culture or your own ability to make change.

Such complicated work in complex environments means that you as a public manager may feel daunted or emboldened by the idea of practicing systemic thinking. You may feel inspired at times or sometimes frustrated. As a public manager, you may already know a great deal about systemic thinking, or this may be your first reading on the topic. Whatever the situation, we offer a pragmatic approach. Throughout this book, we will discuss what is meant by the term systemic thinking, suggest ways to apply systemic thinking, and present tools to support the five practices for creating a vibrant organization.

Systemic Thinking and Sustainability in the Public Sector

Social issues such as reducing income inequality, eliminating human rights abuses, and creating peaceful and effective immigration policies are systemic concerns. Connections among social issues, the natural environment, and day-to-day living have become clearer in recent decades. The United Nations Educational, Scientific and Cultural Organization (UNESCO, 2017) has been at work on educating people about systemic issues for many years and developed 17 Sustainable Development Goals to address the issues. One intention of this book is to support the expansion of such education.

The management of vibrant organizations within the public sector advances Education for Sustainable Development, which is critical to realizing the United Nations' Sustainable Development Goals (UNESCO, 2017). Education for Sustainable Development is typically comprised of three basic elements: CLIMATE, economy, and society (UNESCO, n.d.). Thus far, educational efforts have focused primarily on the topic of climate at the primary, secondary, and postsecondary school levels. We are not arguing that this should change. Rather, we posit that the practice of systemic thinking by public managers within social systems promotes lifelong learning for societal development, thus providing a broader pathway to making meaningful change in systemic issues such as income inequality, racial injustice, and gender inequality, among others.

Systemic thinking functions best when vital perspectives are tapped and shaped toward the transformation of organizations and communities. Sustainable development captures the imagination of dedicated public managers who recognize the connections among the economy, climate, and society as systems. Providing approaches to help guide you as a public manager in your systemic thinking facilitates the inclusive development of people working together as critical contributors, paving the way to new, stronger, and more fluid organizational capacity and sustainability.

Five Practices for Creating a Vibrant Organization

An overview of chapters on the five practices for creating a vibrant organization is described in this section. Although the descriptions follow a chronological order, the book is designed for the reader to start anywhere and obtain value. The chapters are connected intentionally, and in the spirit of design thinking, they are meant to be read and practiced iteratively.

Depicting the system represents an often-revealing practice and is described in Chapter 2. Taking the opportunity to describe the system based on its purpose, functions, and relationships begins a process of shared understanding. Integrating and refining multiple viewpoints is necessary to reflect the complexity of an organizational system. Clarifying the system in terms of a shared view of the system's purpose and how multiple interrelated parts connect and function provides a valuable foundation for dialogue, direction, discovery, and design.

Evaluating the system is described in Chapter 3. Ultimately, the effectiveness of the system is the focal point of evaluation. Effectiveness is more complex than efficiency and addresses the big picture of the system's purpose. In contrast, efficiency is a shorter-term facet of functioning that typically pertains to the process level rather than the system level. Such areas as cost per transaction and speed of transaction are typical focal points of efficiency. Effectiveness, on the other hand, emphasizes how well the system functions in terms of serving the organizational purpose: It requires that each part of the system works well for those served and that the organization consistently improves its ability to deliver more value.

Collaborating within and across systems is discussed in Chapter 4. Effective social systems require a form of connectivity that is proactive, generative, purposeful, and emergence-driven in support of the social system's mission and purpose. Strong connections among people make it possible to marshal resources and apply them to areas that elevate a system's capacity for delivering value. Enlisting contributions from a wide variety of people strengthens the ability of the system to respond to the environment in which it serves.

Developing a systemic culture is the subject of Chapter 5. Helping professionals care deeply about what the organization is dedicated to achieving on behalf of the people who need its services means elevating their voices. Effective social systems benefit from an array of diverse viewpoints based on experience and knowledge that are shared and directed toward system development. Engaging staff in realizing a purpose-driven culture helps elucidate the roles of staff and stakeholders in the creation of a vibrant organization.

Designing a systemic future is the topic of Chapter 6. Systemic thinking asserts the malleability of the social system, recognizing that systems can be designed, redesigned, changed, and transformed. These facets have the power to supercharge an organization to function as it must to remain current, clear, realistic, and responsive to opportunities and challenges. The effective implementation of designs and plans guides the created future into reality.

The Process of Practicing

This book was written for public managers and anyone interested in creating vibrant organizations through the application of systemic thinking. The chapters are arranged with a clear and consistent presentation to promote ease of use. Chapters 2–6 are organized to support the application of each practice and include the following sections.

About the Practice

This section introduces the reader to the practice and provides an overview of the content and systemic thinking approach. How the practice works, the rationale behind it, and the value the practice provides are explained. Ultimately, this section focuses on how the practice supports the application of systemic thinking in a manner that revitalizes the organization.

Theory Box

This section represents a synthesis of the most relevant theoretical foundations that underlie each of the five practices. Emphasis in the Theory Box section is on conceptual vocabulary and abstract ideas relevant to providing practical value. Each theory box contains a concise explanation of systemic thinking concepts (i.e., systems thinking, critical thinking, and design thinking) for reflection and application. When describing systems principles, we cite the original source for each principle whenever possible, so that readers are made aware of the history of various aspects of systems thinking and its progenitors.

Case Study

This section provides two versions of a case study that align with the chapter's topic to support a clearer understanding. Case studies provide practical examples, contrasting the application of traditional public management thinking with systemic thinking. Each case study reveals choices made by public managers in various settings.

Tools

Chapters 2–6 contain multiple tools for use within and across organizations. The tools are designed to support each of the five practices. Each tool was developed using an iterative design-based research process and provides a practical way to enact the concepts emphasized in its respective chapter.

Chapter Summary

This section includes a summary of the chapter's practice and relevant systemic thinking concepts. The chapter summary highlights the value and impact of each practice. Chapter summaries may provide useful reminders about the topics.

Practicing the Practice

This section provides exercises to apply the concepts and tools introduced in each chapter. Practicing the practice underscores the importance of reflection, revision, and taking an iterative approach to systemic thinking and application. This section further emphasizes the importance to public managers of considering approaches, trying them out, revising them, and reflecting with others about the results.

Recommended Reading

Chapters 2–6 include recommendations for further reading. Recommended readings are books, articles, and websites that are theoretical, empirical, or practical in nature. These recommendations provide a resource for expanding one's base of theoretical and practical knowledge associated with each of the practices designed for this book.

Four Steps of Implementation

It is important to note that implementation of the practices outlined in this book is an iterative process. There are four steps that comprise this process: Understanding, Reviewing, Applying, and Reflecting. When practicing any new skill, thought process, or discipline, it is vital first to understand the concepts (Argyris & Schön, 1996). A review of the concepts supports their retention. Applying the learned concepts provides experience, leading to an even greater depth of understanding (Dewey, 2012; National Academies of Sciences, Engineering, and Medicine, 2000). Results occur from these applications, and reflection upon the results provides insights and guides adjustments for future practice (Schön, 1983) and renewed understanding.

The Four Steps of Implementation as they pertain to using this book are described in greater detail below:

1. *Understanding* includes the initial reading of a chapter. It also includes recognizing which components of the chapter the reader grasps and which components of a practice may need further exploration. In practice, understanding includes an evolving comprehension of the problem, situation, or complex system being studied.
2. *Reviewing* includes re-reading a chapter's concepts, tools, and end-of-chapter exercises. It also includes taking a second or third look at any data that may have been collected while practicing a practice (e.g., during interviews with other department heads, employees).
3. *Applying* the concepts learned includes using the tools and practicing the exercises outlined in a chapter. It also includes initiating conversations

or discussions with colleagues and employees about a chapter's practice, concepts, and tools.

4. *Reflecting* encompasses thinking and writing about what occurred as a result of applying the concepts and using the tools. It also includes thinking, writing, and discussing future applications of a concept, tool, or practice.

Of course, the process of implementing systemic thinking may not occur exactly as described here. For example, step three, applying the concepts learned, may require considerable reflection, both individually and with others. Be aware, too, that implementation may be interrupted, forgotten, or taken up again, and may progress perhaps too slowly for the reader's liking. In these instances, we recommend that the reader simply return to this section and begin again with step one, understanding.

In other cases, when implementing a tool or the concepts learned from this book, the results may not be those hoped for or expected. In these instances, we recommend revisiting items two and four (reviewing and reflecting). Put another way, keep in mind that the implementation of a new skill is not a one-and-done phenomenon. Like learning, it is a lifelong pursuit and is typically accomplished iteratively over time. Practice is both the process and the purpose of this book.

References

Argyris, C., & Schön, D. A. (1996). *Organizational learning II: Theory, method, and practice*. Addison-Wesley Publishing Company.

Boardman, J., & Sauser, B. (2013). *Systemic thinking: Building maps for worlds of systems*. John Wiley & Sons.

Buchanan, R. (1992). Wicked problems in design thinking. *Design Issues, 8*(2), 5–21. https://doi.org/10.2307/1511637

Checkland, P. (1999). *Systems thinking, systems practice: Includes a 30-year retrospective*. John Wiley & Sons.

Churchman, C. W. (1968). *The systems approach*. Dell Publishing CO.

Churchman, C. W. (1971). *The design of inquiring systems: Basic concepts of systems and organization*. Basic Books.

Dewey, J. (2012). *Reconstruction in philosophy*. Henry Holt and Company. www.gutenberg.org/ebooks/40089 (Original work published 1920).

Diestler, S. (2020). *Becoming a critical thinker: A user-friendly manual* (7th ed.). Pearson Education.

Gharajedaghi, J. (2011). *Systems thinking: Managing chaos and complexity: A platform for designing business architecture* (3rd ed.). Morgan Kaufmann.

National Academies of Sciences, Engineering, and Medicine. (2000). *How people learn: Brain, mind, experience, and school* [Expanded Edition]. National Academies Press. https://doi.org/10.17226/9853

Nelson, H. G., & Stolterman, E. (2014). *The design way: Intentional change in an unpredictable world*. The MIT Press.

Schön, D. A. (1983). *The reflective practitioner: How professionals think in action.* Basic Books.

Swanson, R. A., & Dobbs, R. L. (2006). The future of systemic and systematic training. *Advances in Developing Human Resources, 8*(4), 548–554. https://doi. org/10.1177/1523422306293012

United Nations Educational, Scientific and Cultural Organization. (n.d.). *Education for sustainable development.* www.unesco.org/en/education-sustainable-development

United Nations Educational, Scientific and Cultural Organization. Division for Inclusion, Peace and Sustainable Development, Education Sector. (2017). *Education for sustainable development goals: Learning objectives.* UNESCO. https:// unesdoc.unesco.org/ark:/48223/pf0000247444

Chapter 2

Depicting the System

Depicting the system means communicating the essence of the organization as a system using a document or visual aid. This may mean describing the system using text, visualizing it using paper and pencil, or using a
basic software program to map the system. For our purposes, we use the
terms depicting, visualizing, mapping, and modeling as synonyms. Depicting the system is the starting place for building a shared understanding of
the organization as a system.

Depicting the *organization* typically means using an organizational
chart: A document or web page that contains titles, positions, and names
of people with lines of authority connecting them vertically and showing
relationships horizontally. Organizational charts are very useful for understanding the hierarchy and knowing who reports to whom, but they do not
include stakeholders or clients, nor do they consider outer environments
(e.g., social, economic, political, ecological) or the organization's purpose.

There are two main approaches to depicting a system: The hard systems
approach and the soft systems approach (Checkland, 1999; Checkland &
Poulter, 2020). The hard systems approach typically involves quantitative metrics that are used to depict simulated resource and output changes
to the system according to managerial decisions (Forrester, 2007). This
approach makes the most sense in private sector organizations that produce and distribute tangible products.

The soft systems approach typically involves qualitative and visual elements that are used to depict a definition of the organization, its processes,
services, relationships, and purpose(s) based on input from employees,
clients, or stakeholders (Checkland, 1999; Checkland & Poulter, 2020).
Checkland (1999) developed the soft systems approach because he found
that many problems faced by managers were much more complex than
expected and not readily solved. As we assert that these types of problems
and complexities often occur in the public sector, this book focuses on
the soft systems approach. Organizational research supports this approach
based on the distinct characteristics of the public sector (Collins, 2005).

DOI: 10.4324/9781003335153-2

A soft systems approach to depiction supports learning and discovery; it often results in a common model of the system that encourages moving beyond routine ways of thinking (Checkland, 1999). Visual and textual descriptions of the system allow for consideration of new possibilities for planning, redesigning, or otherwise improving the organization (Banathy, 1995; Boardman & Sauser, 2013; Gorod et al., 2021). But how do you as a busy public manager reconcile spending time on depicting the system when your job is to manage it? Is there a way to do both and do them well?

About the Practice

An organizational chart depicts the internal hierarchy of an organization, and a system depiction describes the system. The organizational chart does not include all the components of the organization as a system, and the system depiction does not concern itself with internal hierarchies. However, depicting the system integrates multiple perspectives and adds dimension. For example, if you worked at an elementary school and asked for input about the organization as a system, one person might respond that their organization is "A public elementary school," while a second person might describe it as "A place to develop lifelong learners," and a third might say, "This organization serves the community by educating its youth and by providing 250 jobs." While each of the depictions would be correct, once you compared them, you would see that each person's description also seemed incomplete.

Similarly, if you were to ask stakeholders about their role within a system serving youth, you would obtain different responses since different organizations will have distinct perspectives based upon their roles. Depicting a system can provide a broader, more holistic perspective by including diverse views and depicting the relationships between the organization and its partners, stakeholders, and clients. Understanding the relationships and their connection to a system's purpose provides stakeholders with clarity and certainty and supports collaboration and creativity (Regenold & Reed, 2023). For example, when stakeholders see their role within a visual depiction of your system, they are provided context. That visual context may allow them to provide input for planning efforts, suggest ideas for shared grant opportunities, or process your organization's requests more efficiently.

The Process of Depicting the System

The process of depicting the system includes three phases: (1) identifying, (2) defining, and (3) visualizing (Checkland, 1999). The identifying phase is about discerning the components of a system. The defining phase

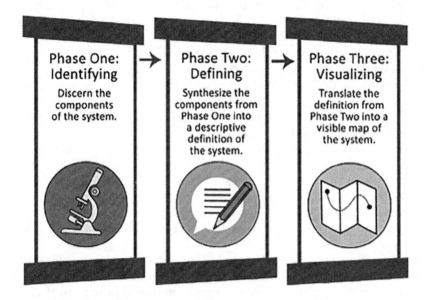

Figure 2.1 The Process of Depicting a System.
Source: Adapted from Checkland (1999)

is about synthesizing the identified components into a clear and comprehensive definition of the system. The visualizing phase is about translating the textual definition into a visible map of the system.

It is not necessary to complete all three phases of the process to depict your system. Depicting your system may mean only using the identification phase or stopping once you have a definition of your system. Or you may choose to complete all three phases to depict your system visually (see Figure 2.1).

Phase One: Identifying

Identifying the components of your system is performed using CATWOE Analysis (Checkland, 1999). CATWOE is an acronym that stands for Clients (or customers), Actors (or employees), the process of Transformation, the Worldview of members of the system, Oversight of the system, and constraints from the system's larger Environment (i.e., political, social, ecological, and economic factors influencing the system). To identify the components of your system, simply use the acronym as a guide (see Figure 2.2, The CATWOE Analysis Tool).

To be more specific about the meaning of the acronym CATWOE (Checkland, 1999):

- **Clients** of the system are those receiving services.
- **Actors** are those performing services.
- The process of **Transformation** is a description of what you do for clients.
- The **Worldview** of the system is the overall perspective of the organization that may inform the organizational vision. A worldview is a belief that guides an organization toward fulfilling its mission or purpose. A worldview is often positive. For example, the worldview might be that it is an honor to serve or that humility is humanity's best resource.
- **Oversight** of the system is typically provided by one or more levels above the organizational system. For example, if the system is a local government organization, oversight might be provided by a state-level agency.
- Finally, constraints from the system's larger **Environment** are effects felt within the organization that come from influences outside the organization. Examples of environmental constraints might include an election resulting in a new administration with different values from those held by the previous administration; or an economic recession during which thousands of people lose their jobs. Such environmental constraints would likely force the organization to change its course of action.

The integration of CATWOE Analysis (Checkland, 1999) with management practices occurs incrementally. Begin by doing an analysis on your own, then ask your direct reports, colleagues, and other stakeholders to complete the analysis from their perspectives. Allow time for people to reflect and return their analyses to you; then allow time to review and reflect on all the input.

Sharing the identification phase in this way provides others the opportunity to think about the organization as a system, to reflect on mutual clients and the process of providing services, and to consider the influences of oversight and various environments. It also begins the process of relating to others in a more systemic, collaborative, and inclusive way. Showing respect for others' views, responsibilities, and contributions helps you begin to depict your system and shape it. More details about this phase can be found in the Tools section of this chapter.

Phase Two: Defining

A system definition transcends the organizational chart by directing focus toward the organization's mission or purpose. Yet system definitions do not stop there. A system definition includes its purposes, employees, partners, stakeholders, clients, relationships, constraints on the system, and the process of transformation that client services provide.

Developing a system definition is an iterative process that can be conducted in short bursts over a longer timeframe. In other words, the defining phase can be completed incrementally to complement your work as a public manager rather than add to it. Defining your system builds upon the work you and others performed in the identification phase. It involves synthesizing the data collected from that phase and developing a descriptive, comprehensive paragraph from those data.

To be more specific, the process of synthesizing the data collected from the CATWOE Analyses (Checkland, 1999) you and others completed begins with grouping all of the "C" data about your system's clients into one document. Next, group the "A" data together in the same document, and do the same with the "T" data, and so on. For example, imagine that you first collected CATWOE Analysis data from 18 people in your organization using the CATWOE tool from the tools section of this chapter. You would then have 18 written descriptions about who your clients are, 18 descriptions of who the actors are, 18 descriptions of what the process of transformation is like, and so on.

Once all of the data are grouped together in one format and place (e.g., in a spreadsheet), you can begin to synthesize it. Synthesis is simply a matter of recognizing and naming themes, patterns, commonalities, or emergent possibilities in what people said about each CATWOE Analysis item (Checkland, 1999). Write your synthesis of each CATWOE item in a separate column next to the original data you collected; try to keep the synthesis of each CATWOE item to one sentence. The benefit of synthesizing data is that it calls for the creation of a new, collaborative whole from several individual contributions. In other words, synthesis calls for and prompts design thinking—an aspect of systemic thinking.

See Table 2.1 for a brief example of data collected and synthesized for a CATWOE Analysis of a public workforce development system. Each sentence in the left-hand column of Table 2.1, entitled "Original Data Collected," is an example of written statements received from six colleagues, direct reports, or executives throughout a public workforce development system. Each of the sentences in the right-hand column is an example of a synthesis conducted by a public manager after collecting those data. (Data collected includes only the first three elements of CATWOE: Clients, Actors, and the process of Transformation, as an example of synthesizing.)

After completing the synthesis, transfer each of your synthesized statements to a document to be developed into a system definition. Since there are six items in CATWOE (Checkland, 1999), it's likely you will have six sentences. You will arrange these six sentences into a single paragraph.

Table 2.1 Example Data Collection and Synthesized Statements.

Original Data Collected	Synthesized Statements
"C" data: Clients (Customers)	**"C" Data: Clients (Customers)**
People who need help finding jobs. Businesses who need help finding employees. Our customers are the people who walk through our doors. Clients are human beings down on their luck. The people we serve through our programs and services. Our clients are the employers and potential employees who use our services.	Our clients include jobseekers and businesses.
"A" data: Actors (Employees)	**"A" Data: Actors (Employees)**
We provide career counseling. We offer several services to both businesses and people seeking employment. We contact businesses to educate them about our services We deliver training to jobseekers on writing resumes and other job-readiness skills We partner with providers who serve vulnerable populations. We work with elected officials, community, and business leaders, to help solve our workforce and economic development issues.	We educate and support businesses and people seeking jobs.
"T" data: Transformation process	**"T" data: Transformation process**
It's a slow process with many obstacles, but we get there eventually. If more employers would use incumbent-worker training, the process would be a lot better. By guiding jobseekers along career pathways and supporting their choices. By working with employers to identify their needs and filling them. Through partnerships with the right organizations. Alignment of service delivery and support of individual entrepreneurship and creativity.	Integrating the needs of businesses and individuals strengthens workforce development.

Source: Adapted from Regenold (2020)

Finally, we recommend creating three versions of a system definition (or three distinct paragraphs) that you will show to others. To create distinct versions, try arranging the sentences in a different order. To do this, you might begin each paragraph with a different CATWOE element. For example:

1. The first version of a defining paragraph might begin with a synthesized sentence about Clients.
2. The second version might begin with a sentence about Oversight.
3. And the third version might begin with a sentence about Actors.

Once you have created three versions, select the one that you think is the best representation of your system. Then ask at least two other people to vote for the definition they think best represents the system. The version that receives the most votes is your System Definition. More details about this phase can be found in the Tools section of this chapter.

Phase Three: Visualizing

When depicting your system, you have the option of stopping at the second phase, defining, or even after the initial phase of identifying system components. As not everyone will be interested in taking the third step of visualizing their system, completing the first or second phase of the depiction process is perfectly acceptable. However, for those who wish to see their system definition take shape graphically as a system map or model, the phase of visualizing will be especially informative and appealing.

Visualizing in this context means taking the system definition created in Phase two and translating it into a system map consisting of bits of text, shapes, lines, and colors. The translation of text into visual format occurs by breaking the system definition text into parts and connecting those parts using shapes and lines. The procedure is similar to creating your own jigsaw puzzle pieces. In this situation, when the puzzle is put back together, the picture will truly be a whole greater than the sum of its pieces. Visual depictions of this type are useful for sharing and discussing complex systems, concepts, and ideas (Khansari et al., 2016; Sauser et al., 2011).

We recommend sharing your visual system depiction with staff and stakeholders and encouraging them to provide suggestions for improvement (Boardman & Sauser, 2013; Checkland, 1999). Take notes on what they suggest and update your system diagram accordingly. Suggestions made by people who know your system often enhance the system's depiction, benefiting future viewers. More details about the depiction process and examples of system mapping are provided in the Tools section of this chapter.

Depicting a system may begin as an individual exercise, but it quickly calls for the involvement of others. Other managers, employees, and leaders are excellent sources of information about the organization as a system. Clients and other stakeholders may also be consulted, and they often provide useful perspectives about what your system means to them. Sharing the depiction process with employees, clients, and other stakeholders is a beneficial and rewarding experience that fosters collaboration and communication. Taking an incremental approach to depiction is an effective way to manage people while engaging in the practice.

Box 2.1   Theory Box: Depicting the System.

A systemic thinking approach to depicting the system supports the inclusion of system stakeholders, showing relevant relationships, processes, and purposes, as well as worldviews and constraints from the environment. The practice of depicting the system relies on active listening, striving for understanding, and the willing contribution and reception of feedback. Systems thinking principles, critical thinking aspects, and design thinking aspects relevant to depicting a system are described below.

Systems Thinking Principles

Systems thinking principles were derived from original sources whenever possible. We used original sources to incorporate the history of systems thinking and to acknowledge the progenitors of the principles. The following systems thinking principles support the practice of depicting the system:

- *Boundary.* The systems principle of boundary pertains to the definition and description of the system as distinct from the environment(s) in which the system operates. System boundaries represent an abstraction that guides understanding and shapes ways of organizing. There are different ways of bounding the system. For example, a state government might be the system in focus. On a smaller scale, the system under consideration might be a city government. Drilling down further, the system of focus might be a department within a specific municipal organization. In system depiction, the boundary is set around the area where the transformation process occurs—the area outside that transformational process is considered to be that system's environment (Checkland, 1999; Churchman, 1971).

- *Complementarity.* The systems principle of complementarity suggests that there are multiple perspectives for any given system. Each viewpoint is both correct and incomplete, yet it enriches whole-system understanding by providing insights from distinct vantage points (Bohr, 1928). Integrating multiple viewpoints of staff, management, leadership, and other stakeholders helps ensure accuracy and inclusivity, thereby strengthening the decisions made on behalf of the system.
- *Holism.* The systems principle of holism means that the system must be considered as a whole rather than a sum of its parts (Smuts, 1927). The characteristics of the whole exceed the value that is created by merely collecting or adding together the parts of a system. Consideration of the whole often yields insights not available by perceiving the organization as an aggregation of parts.
- *System Purpose.* System purpose refers to the reason that the organization exists (Beer, 2002; Checkland, 1999). In the public sector, system purpose refers to the *legally authorized* reason that the organization exists.[1] System purpose is at the core of what the organization delivers. Clarity of purpose is vital to the interests of all members of the system and to those it serves. Alignment around the system purpose is critical to effective performance.

Critical Thinking Aspects

Critical thinking supports the depiction of a system by using discernment and judgment to help identify boundaries and other components of the system. Critical thinking further benefits the depiction of a system by using logic and reasoning to support the inclusion of all members of the system. The following critical thinking aspects support the depiction of a system:

- Determine the point(s) at which inputs come into the system from the environment.
- Determine the point(s) at which outputs leave the system and enter the environment.
- Identify the department, agency, or level of government responsible for the process of transformation within the system.
- Identify the other elements of CATWOE Analysis that comprise the system.

Design Thinking Aspects

While critical thinking supports discernment of the parts of a system, design thinking supports the synthesis of those parts into a cohesive whole (Buchanan, 1992; Gharajedaghi, 2011; Nelson & Stolterman, 2014). When depicting the organizational system, design thinking supports the bringing together of diverse ideas and suggestions about what the system is and does. The following design thinking aspects support the depiction of a system:

- Notice the language people at work use to describe your organization.
- Pay attention to how your organization uses visuals (maps, models, charts, graphs, etc.) to depict complexity.
- Identify contrasting elements that might be brought together in new or creative ways (e.g., CATWOE Analysis components collected from several employees or stakeholders).
- Notice how the system parts and relationships connect with the system purpose (e.g., in conversations with employees and stakeholders).

Note: [1]Typically, an organization's purpose is synonymous with its mission, while an organization's vision is a description of what life will look like once the mission/purpose has been fulfilled.

Case Study: A College Dean Struggles With Planning in a Rural District

This case study compares two managers' approaches to an issue in the context of higher education. The first manager uses traditional, analytical thinking, or a "non-systemic approach." The second manager may use traditional, analytical thinking, but importantly also uses systemic thinking, or a "systemic approach." The non-systemic approach stops short of recognizing the wholeness and complexity of a social system. The systemic approach recognizes the breadth and depth of the educational mission of the college.

Non-systemic Approach

After a fraught situation with a difficult dean, the board of a rural college district appointed a student services professional to act as interim academic dean. The interim dean remained in that temporary position for nearly two years without being offered the regular position. During this time, a department head committed to leading strategic planning sessions with his core planning team for the college faculty and staff.

Early in the initiative, the department head arranged a meeting with the interim dean to share the direction of the planning endeavor. The department head had expressed to the core planning team his excitement about sharing with the interim dean the plan to involve all staff and stakeholders in planning and preliminary interviews, including those who provided support services to students. The department head knew the importance of support services—that many students in the college district were low-income and had benefitted from meal plans, housing, and health services, including mental health.

The department head was especially eager to involve staff and stakeholders in preliminary interviews to build what he considered a whole-system approach. He recognized that no department involves faculty alone but includes a more complex array of resources and people with expertise. Early in the project, the department head and core planning team formed a bond around the idea of helping everyone in the organization see that they were "all one thing" and existed to help students learn and support them throughout their academic careers.

The meeting with the interim dean surprised the department head and the core planning team. The interim dean expressed deep concern about involving everyone. He indicated that he would like to preapprove anyone being considered for involvement in interviews or strategic planning. As the department head specified by name support staff and provider partners working with the school, the interim dean immediately shot back a veto for involving certain participants.

Although somewhat dispirited, the department head and core planning team proceeded to meet with the people whom the interim dean approved to include. The department head and the core planning team set up warm and welcoming meetings with groups of staff, seeking to work with people to build a visual depiction of the organization as a system. During the initial meeting, it became clear that there were two groups of people: Those wanting to take part and answer questions openly, and those who were reporting back to the interim dean any perceived threats or negativity about potential changes.

When discussing how the system might be made visual, a few of the participants exclaimed, "We have an organizational chart, and that's all we need." The department head and team responded that the organizational chart served one purpose, while the system visual revealed the connectivity of the numerous parts of the system, all of which were directed at accomplishing one primary mission: Helping students learn with needed supports.

It became clear very quickly that there was strong resistance by the interim dean to engaging in conversations about systemic connections among parts of the educational enterprise. It was further evident that the interim dean was likely rewarding resistors of the effort and that any attempt to unify people was not seen as desirable. Given the strong resistance to involving all stakeholders and staff in the preliminary discussions and interviews as well as planning activities, the department head determined that the project should not proceed as planned. Resistance from the top meant a lack of authorization that thwarted productive participation.

Systemic Approach

The board of a rural college district experienced a challenging situation with its dean and released him from service. The board decided to appoint an individual who was well respected as a department head at the college to act as interim dean. The person who had served as a department head was known for showing respect to staff, stakeholders, and students.

The college board informed the interim dean of an opportunity for her in this position to guide the development of a new strategic plan. The board indicated that this endeavor potentially had great value for bringing the college and departments together after strife based on concerns in the previous administration. The interim dean agreed and took up the challenge of working with the core planning team, representing multiple stakeholders and educators. The college board members agreed to participate in the strategic planning and preliminary processes as needed. They voiced their support of the interim dean's agreement to "lead the charge" to help the district build a substantial strategic plan that would speak to families and all members of the system.

The interim dean conducted several initial meetings with the core planning team, who shared information about the vast array of support services provided by stakeholders to families of students. Both the core planning team and the interim dean were accustomed to working with a diverse array of people in rural areas and expressed respect for all students. The interim dean and the core planning team worked together to identify all the people who could be involved in strategic planning, notably at the earliest stages of the initiative.

During an extensive sequence of meetings with the board, administration, staff, and stakeholders, the core planning team found themselves buoyed up by the willingness of people to respond directly and completely to questions. Most impressive was the sense of commitment shared by faculty and staff who worked with students, as well as those providers of student support services. It became clear that a sense of community was developing in the core planning team as it interacted with staff and stakeholders.

One of the preliminary efforts was to "map" what the system looked like. The core planning team and interim dean shared with all people interviewed that their viewpoints were absolutely necessary for building a picture of "who we are" and "what we do." In the words of the interim dean, "No one of us can do this big job alone. We need one another, and the students need us all."

The visual picture that emerged showed a great deal of complexity. Some people said it was a spiderweb, but it was an interesting one that seemed complete. One major viewpoint discussed was: How can we make sure that everyone understands that this picture will change over time? We need to agree to keep growing stronger and more connected to do what we are here to do.

It became clear immediately that people in the organization believed that education consisted of much more than faculty members teaching. The vast majority of people who participated in early focus groups and interviews expressed that they understood the importance of their role and the roles of others as connected to shaping students' lives in a rewarding and productive way. The emergent worldview was that education had the power to transform people and the community.

Collaborative work by the core planning team in partnership with the board and interim dean revealed the importance for all system partners of visually depicting the organization as a system. Based on the positive interaction, participants agreed that developing a visual picture of the system added value. Several of the participants voiced the following message, "It really helps to picture what we do together to make education better for our community."

Tools

The three tools provided in this chapter were designed to support the practice of depicting a system:

1. The CATWOE Analysis Tool.
2. Four Steps to Developing a System Definition Tool.
3. Eight Rules for Visualizing Your System Definition Tool.

Each tool supports one phase of the depiction process. The CATWOE Analysis Tool supports Phase one, identifying. The four steps to developing a System Definition Tool supports Phase two, defining. And the eight rules for visualizing your System Definition Tool supports Phase three, visualizing.

CATWOE Analysis Tool

Being able to identify the primary components of your system is the beginning of a deeper understanding of your organization as a system. Recognizing and explicitly describing each element of CATWOE (Checkland, 1999) make it possible to identify your own and others' perspectives about your system simultaneously. In other words, using the CATWOE Analysis Tool to identify system components helps you as a public manager collaborate to depict your system. See Figure 2.2.

CATWOE ANALYSIS TOOL

CATWOE is an acronym based on Peter Checkland's (1999) work that is used to identify the parts of your system.

Instructions: Read the Categories of Analysis section and answer the Questions for Reflection. Write answers in the corresponding Responses section.

Categories of Analysis	Questions for Reflection	Responses
Clients: Primary clients or customers receiving services.	1. Who are the clients or customers of your system?	
Actors: The employees serving the customers.	2. What actions are taken to deliver the organization's services to clients?	
Transformation process: The change from inputs (e.g., resources) to outputs and outcomes (e.g., results).	3. How does the transformation of inputs to outputs and outcomes occur?	
Worldview: The beliefs and values that underlie your organizational system's culture.	4. How does the worldview reinforce (or obstruct) the system's purpose(s)?	
Oversight:* ‡ The authorizing agent for your system; the body that provides or denies resources.	5. How does oversight connect with the system?	
Environmental constraints: Political, social, ecological, or economic issues outside your system that affect it.	6. How do environmental constraints change the operations, culture, or performance of your system?	

*The "O" in Checkland's (1999) CATWOE stands for "Owner." We changed this to "Oversight" because if there were an owner of a public organization it would be the public, and it may not be feasible to include the public in a system depiction.

‡ Identification of Oversight depends on how you bound the system. For example, if you are part of a team within a state-level agency that is a part of a region, the Oversight might be the larger department, the state-level agency, the region, an elected official or legislature, or a higher-level government, depending on the level of analysis (system boundary) you choose to depict.

Figure 2.2 CATWOE Analysis Tool.

Source: Adapted from Checkland (1999)

Other Potential Uses of the CATWOE Analysis Tool

- As a collaborative feedback tool to gain necessary, important input from employees and other stakeholders of your system.
- As an educational tool to show new employees, potential partners, and existing stakeholders what the system is about.
- As a regulatory tool for setting common standards within multiple-organization partnerships.
- As an organizing tool to identify and understand the most important aspects of a new project, what it intends to accomplish, and for whom.

Four Steps to Developing a System Definition Tool

The next tool builds upon the work completed using the CATWOE Analysis (Checkland, 1999) Tool in the identification phase. The purpose of developing a system definition is to share a cohesive, comprehensive statement about your system with your employees, clients, and other stakeholders. Collecting and synthesizing the data from your and others' CATWOE Analyses allows you to integrate important perspectives about the system. Developing a system definition helps you share the synthesized data from the CATWOE Analysis. This synthesis, in the form of a system definition, communicates an inclusive, holistic depiction of your system. See Figure 2.3.

Other Potential Uses of the Developing a System Definition Tool

- As a tool to begin the development of systemic collaborations with those in your organization or outside of it.
- As a tool to develop your ability to synthesize and create holistic perspectives.
- As a tool to help with the writing of disparity statements required in some grant applications or with the writing of purpose statements for projects.

Eight Rules for Visualizing Your System Definition Tool

The third tool in this chapter helps to take your system definition developed in Phase two and turn it into a visual depiction of your system. The main purpose of depicting a system visually is to convey complexity in a clear and simple way. While not everyone may initially appreciate or understand a visual, system diagrams, maps, or models often help people grasp complexity more rapidly. Viewing a system as well as reading about it prompts dialogue about the system: Ways it could be improved, how planning might occur, ways that relationships could be strengthened, or

FOUR STEPS TO DEVELOPING A
SYSTEM DEFINITION TOOL

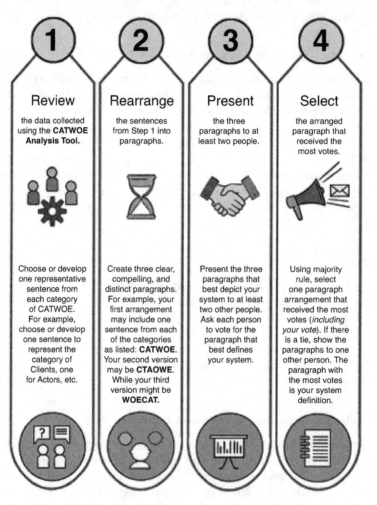

1	**2**	**3**	**4**
Review	**Rearrange**	**Present**	**Select**
the data collected using the **CATWOE Analysis Tool.**	the sentences from Step 1 into paragraphs.	the three paragraphs to at least two people.	the arranged paragraph that received the most votes.
Choose or develop one representative sentence from each category of CATWOE. For example, choose or develop one sentence to represent the category of Clients, one for Actors, etc.	Create three clear, compelling, and distinct paragraphs. For example, your first arrangement may include one sentence from each of the categories as listed: **CATWOE**. Your second version may be **CTAOWE**. While your third version might be **WOECAT.**	Present the three paragraphs that best depict your system to at least two other people. Ask each person to vote for the paragraph that best defines your system.	Using majority rule, select one paragraph arrangement that received the most votes (*including your vote*). If there is a tie, show the paragraphs to one other person. The paragraph with the most votes is your system definition.

Figure 2.3 Four Steps to Developing a System Definition Tool.

Source: Adapted from Checkland (1999)

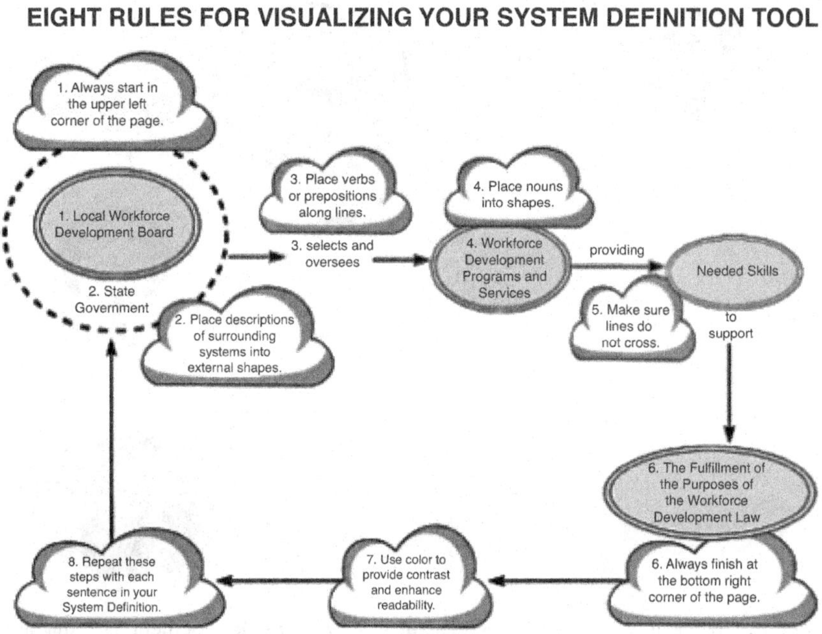

EIGHT RULES FOR VISUALIZING YOUR SYSTEM DEFINITION TOOL

Figure 2.4 Eight Rules for Visualizing Your System Definition Tool.

Source: Adapted from Boardman & Sauser (2013)

ways that the system might be redesigned. In other words, visually depicting your system provides many opportunities for creativity, design thinking, critical thinking, communication, and collaboration.

The Eight Rules for Visualizing Your System Definition Tool are displayed in Figure 2.4. Working from the upper left corner of the page, take the first sentence of your system definition and break it into parts: NOUNS, verbs, and prepositional phrases. Map those parts onto the page using shapes, text boxes, and lines. Follow this process with each sentence of your system definition, working your way toward the bottom right corner of the page, ultimately leading toward fulfillment of the system's purpose(s).

Examples of system diagrams known as systemigrams (Boardman & Sauser, 2013) may be seen in Figures 2.5–2.9. Systemigrams may be developed using a free software program available online. The software is called SystemiTool, and it is freely available at the Systems Engineering Research Center at the Stevens Institute of Technology. Visit the website, *https:// sercuarc.org/serc-tools/*, and scroll to the middle of the page to gain access to the SystemiTool. Users may download either Windows or Mac versions or use a web-based version of the tool.

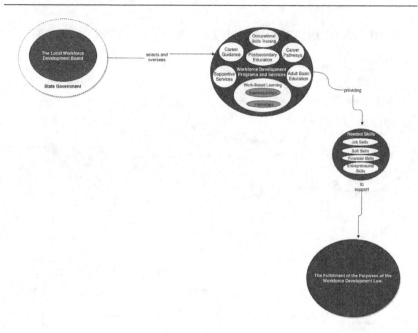

Figure 2.5 Example of an Initial Strand of a Public Workforce Development Systemigram.

Source: Adapted from Regenold (2020)

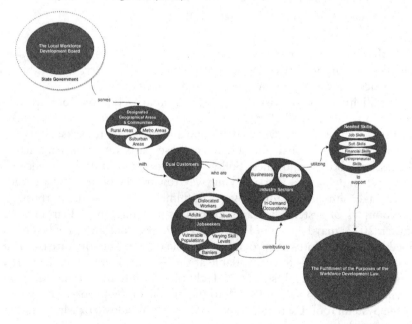

Figure 2.6 Example of the Second Strand of a Public Workforce Development Systemigram.

Source: Adapted from Regenold (2020)

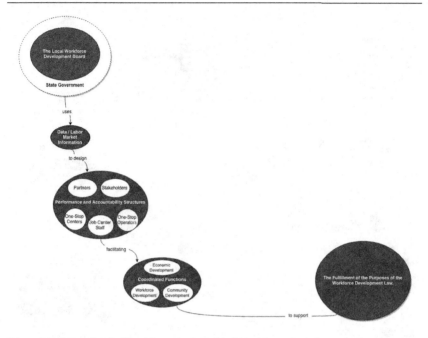

Figure 2.7 Example of a Third Strand of a Public Workforce Development Systemigram.

Source: Adapted from Regenold (2020)

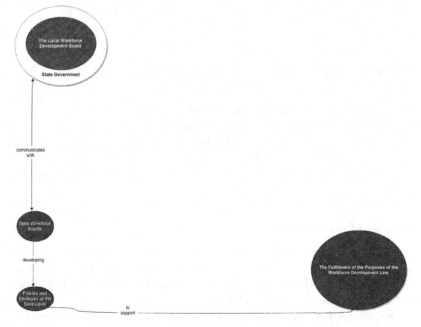

Figure 2.8 Example of a Fourth Strand of a Public Workforce Development Systemigram.

Source: Adapted from Regenold (2020)

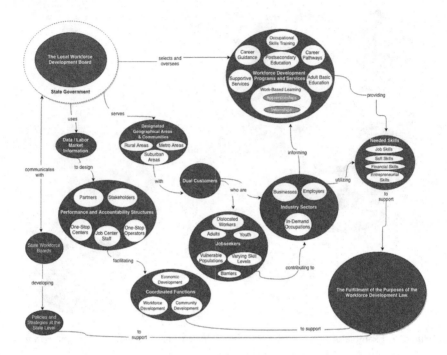

Figure 2.9 Example of Whole Systemigram of the Public Workforce Development System.

Source: Adapted from Regenold (2020)

Other Potential Uses of Eight Rules for Visualizing Your System Definition Tool

- As a writing tool for crafting simple messages.
- As an issue-identification tool for identifying ways to influence the use of resources, identifying gaps within the system, and identifying the relationships that need to be strengthened.
- As an idea-generation tool or strategic-planning tool to improve the system.

Examples of System Mapping

System maps, models, or diagrams may be created using pencil and paper, the aforementioned free software program called SystemiTool (Systems Engineering Research Center, n.d.), or any other visualization software the reader desires. Some people prefer to begin sketching their diagram using paper and pencil first, then use a software program. It should be noted that using software to map your system makes it easy to share, edit, or update results.

It is important to keep in mind that models are not one-to-one representations of a system; they are an abstract interpretation of the system. Due to the homomorphic nature of models and the dynamic nature of systems, updating or revising your system map on a regular basis is encouraged. That may mean updating annually, semi-annually, or quarterly, depending on the nature of your work and your system's environment.

Boardman and Sauser (2013) urge creators of system maps to present them to viewers one strand at a time before presenting the whole system diagram. Doing so allows people to take in what the depiction is about without being overwhelmed. When walking viewers through how the diagram is read, start from the upper left corner of the diagram and finish at the bottom right corner.

Figure 2.5 is an example of an initial strand depicting a public workforce development system. The strand may be read as follows: The Local Workforce Development Board selects and oversees Workforce Development Programs and Services (such as occupational skills training, career guidance, postsecondary education) providing needed skills (such as job skills, soft skills) to support the fulfillment of the purposes of the Workforce Development Law.

You may find that showing your diagram to staff and stakeholders encourages them to provide suggestions for improvement. For example, in the top right section of Figure 2.5, elements such as "occupational skills training," "career guidance," and "postsecondary education," were suggested by stakeholders to provide viewers with examples of Workforce Development Programs and Services (Regenold, 2020). Including stakeholders' suggestions enriches the system depiction and helps other viewers to see more readily the whole picture of what the system is and does.

The second strand of the visualized system definition is the next piece to share with employees and other stakeholders. An example is shown in Figure 2.6. This example strand may be read as follows: The Local Workforce Development Board (overseen by the State Government) serves designated geographical areas and communities with dual customers who are job seekers contributing to industry sectors (such as businesses and employers) utilizing needed skills to support the fulfillment of the Workforce Development Law.

An example of the third strand of the system diagram is shown in Figure 2.7. This example strand may be read as follows: The Local Workforce Development Board (overseen by the State Government) uses data and labor market information to design performance and accountability structures (such as one-stop centers, one-stop operators) facilitating coordinated functions to support the fulfillment of the Workforce Development Law.

An example of the final strand of the systemigram is shown in Figure 2.8. This example strand may be read as follows: The Local Workforce Development Board (overseen by the State Government) communicates with State Workforce Boards developing policies and strategies at the state level to support the fulfillment of the Workforce Development Law.

Finally, show viewers the whole systemigram and let them review it. An example of an entire system map based on a system definition is shown in Figure 2.9. Having already seen the system map one strand at a time, viewers of the whole visual depiction of the system are more likely to take it in and may begin to think of ways to use the depiction to improve the system.

As a reminder, system maps, models, or diagrams may be developed using paper and pencil or any visualization software the reader chooses. The purpose of developing a visualization of the system definition is to provide staff, clients, and other stakeholders with the opportunity to see and discuss the nature of the system and suggest ways to improve it. Keep in mind that using shapes within shapes is a good way to depict complexity. Following the Eight Rules for Visualizing Your System Definition Tool in Figure 2.4 will guide you in depicting your system clearly and completely.

Chapter Summary

Depicting the system begins with identifying the parts that comprise the system by obtaining feedback from internal or external stakeholders. Next, the parts of the system are synthesized into a system definition consisting of a paragraph of text. Finally, the system is visualized using paper and pencil or computer software. Each phase of depiction builds upon the next, but you as a public manager may choose to complete only the initial identification phase or you may also complete the definition phase. Depicting the system is most effectively accomplished by combining it with other management opportunities such as collaborating within and across systems. Visualizing the system provides many additional benefits, but it is not required to depict the system.

However the system is depicted, you as a public manager have the opportunity to generate a clear rendering of your complex social system and to orchestrate with others a deep understanding of it. That depiction portrays the complexity and simplicity of a social system. Complexity is indicated by the multiple stakeholders, service providers, business and community leaders, in addition to staff, supervisors, and managers within the main public organization itself. Simplicity is expressed by the system's purpose(s) authorized by law. Depicting the system provides numerous emergent ways for you to improve the system that would not have become readily available without the use of the depiction process.

Practicing the Practice

Several suggestions are provided to help you expand the practice of depicting the system. Practice provides an incremental way to implement ideas. Each exercise was designed to support a phase of depicting the system: Identifying, defining, and visualizing.

Exploring Approaches to Depicting the System (See Case Study)

An important aspect of your role as a public manager is to engage staff and stakeholders in describing the organizational system. Describing the system supports the development and documentation of a clear and agreed-upon definition of the system that reflects multiple viewpoints. Enlisting staff to analyze the case studies provides professional development in synthesizing systems thinking, critical thinking, and design thinking of collaborative partners to represent the current system accurately and comprehensively.

1. Review the Non-Systemic Approach in the Case Study section during a meeting and pose these questions:

   a. How would you describe the way staff, clients, and other stakeholders might have reacted to the way the interim dean or department head handled the opportunity to depict the organizational system?
   b. What are the benefits and drawbacks to the non-systemic approach to depicting the organization?
   c. To what extent did this approach build commitment to a common purpose?

2. Request that meeting participants read the Systemic Approach in the Case Study section, and pose the following questions:

   a. How would you describe the way staff, clients, and other stakeholders might have reacted to the way the interim dean handled the opportunity to depict the organizational system?
   b. What are some of the potential benefits and drawbacks of the systemic approach to depicting the system?
   c. Who in our organizational system needs to be included in the depiction of the system?

Identifying the Elements of Your System (See Table 2.1 and Figure 2.2)

This exercise was developed to supplement the use of the CATWOE Analysis Tool.

It is important to recognize that describing your system is enriched by gaining multiple perspectives from people within the system. Applying the

CATWOE Analysis Tool provides a useful way to clarify the parts of your system.

1. Independently answer each question in the CATWOE Analysis Tool. This will help you gain familiarity with the tool and recognize the benefit of including others' perspectives.
2. Meet one-on-one with five to seven staff members you want to invite to complete the CATWOE Analysis Tool. Ideally, include people at different levels of authority and from different departments.
3. Explain to each person that the CATWOE Analysis Tool offers a way to capture each person's understanding of the system. Each completed CATWOE Analysis Tool will be used to shape consensus about the nature of the organization as a system.
4. Collect the completed CATWOE Analyses from participants, and summarize all original data, as shown in the first column of Table 2.1.
5. Reconvene the group and show your incomplete table to the group.
6. Assign the group to create synthesized sentences, as shown in the second column of Table 2.1.
7. Pose the following questions to the group:

   a. How does use of the CATWOE Analysis Tool change your perspective of our system?
   b. What new ideas does using this tool reveal about our system?
   c. As we continue to evolve as a system, what other people or organizations need to be included to help us represent the whole system?

Developing Your System Definition (See Figure 2.3)

This exercise was developed to supplement the use of the Four Steps to Developing a System Definition Tool. The CATWOE Analysis Tool provides the basis for shaping a system definition for your organizational system. The results from performing a CATWOE Analysis generate a set of statements for each of the categories (Clients, Actors, etc.) that will comprise a paragraph that defines the system.

The sequence in which the sentences are presented reveals a particular way of looking at the system. It is important to recognize that different members of the system may perceive the system according to their roles, which is perfectly acceptable. For instance, the Actors (employees) who deliver the services may begin the paragraph by stating what the Actors do, based on their perspective. This would be different from a paragraph that begins with Customers, for instance.

1. Using the data collected from the CATWOE Analysis Tool, create one synthesized sentence from each of the categories of CATWOE. If you followed the instructions in step six of the CATWOE section above, you

have already completed this step. Create a paragraph that includes all the sentences representing the CATWOE categories. Note the order of your sentences—which element was represented first, second, third, etc.

2. Arrange the sentences into a different, second configuration, for example: WOECAT. Beginning with a different category changes the nature of the system definition. The purpose of resequencing the sentences is to create a paragraph that reflects the system from a different viewpoint, for example, the Worldview, the Oversight, the Environment, to shape a view of the system.

3. Develop a third paragraph arrangement. This may, for instance, be CTAOEW, reflecting yet another perspective of the system. We recommend only using three paragraphs since using more variations may become unwieldy.

4. Now that you have three distinct paragraphs, review them. Decide for yourself on the one that best represents your system.

5. Show the three paragraphs to at least two different people, asking them which best defines your system.

6. The paragraph that receives the most votes, including your vote, is your system definition.

7. Bring together the people who may have an interest in the system definition, and pose the following questions to the group:

   a. How does the system definition help you understand our system?

   b. How do you think this system definition could help clients appreciate how our system works?

   c. How could this system definition help our partners and providers recognize their roles in our system?

Visualizing Your System (See Figure 2.4)

This exercise was developed to supplement the use of the Eight Rules for Visualizing Your System Definition Tool. Creating a visual picture of your system means taking the system definition developed above and breaking the system definition into text, shapes, and colors, and connecting them with lines and arrows. In effect, you are building a puzzle from known parts to create a picture that represents the whole as greater than the sum of those independent parts. Complex social systems can be difficult to understand when only text is used. Therefore, building a picture allows for greater appeal and buy-in by everyone associated with the system.

1. Using the system definition, take the first sentence and break it into parts: Nouns, verbs, and prepositional phrases.

2. Start at the top left of the page and place the main noun in a circle. Place verbs or prepositions along the lines.

3. Connect the verbs or prepositions to the next circle, and place the next noun in that circle.
4. Follow the same practice with each sentence of your system definition.
5. As you work through drawing the definition, make sure that the lines do not cross one another.
6. Work toward the bottom right of the page, where you show the purpose of the system in its own circle.
7. Show your visual depiction of the system to staff and stakeholders and ask the following questions:

   a. How accurate is this picture?
   b. What else needs to be included?
   c. Make notes of the suggestions received.

8. Revise your system diagram to incorporate the input you received in Step 7.
9. After revising your system diagram, review it with staff and stakeholders and pose the following question: What should be changed in our actual system to support our purpose more effectively?

Reflecting on Practicing the Practice

Reflection on the practice of depicting the system deepens understanding and can lead to further insights. Thinking about, writing about, and discussing the chapter, using the tools, and practicing the practice reveals new perspectives, connections, and opportunities to serve. Reflecting can take place as an individual or group activity. Consider the following questions and write or discuss your responses:

1. What worked about the practice of depicting the system?
2. What did not work about the practice?
3. What did you notice about your own thinking during the practice?
4. What did you notice about the interactions and behaviors of others?
5. What changes in understanding of the system occurred as a result of practicing this practice?
6. What might you do differently the next time you practice this practice?

Recommended Readings

On Visualization in Strategic Planning and Management

Eppler, M. J., & Platts, K. W. (2009). Visual strategizing: The systematic use of visualization in the strategic-planning process. *Long Range Planning, 42*(1), 42–74. https://doi.org/10.1016/j.lrp.2008.11.005

Eppler and Platts studied the reasons for using visuals in strategic management processes such as analyzing data, creating plans, or implementing projects. We chose this article because of its clear exposition of the benefits of using visuals in management.

On an Early Use of Visuals in Management

Yates, J. (1985). Graphs as a managerial tool: A case study of Du Pont's use of graphs in the early twentieth century. *International Journal of Business Communication, 22*(1), 5–33. https://doi.org/10.1177/002194368502200101

Yates conducted a historical case study of the conglomerate Du Pont and its use of graphs in business operations from the early 1900s to 1949. She described the emergent need for graphs as one that arose from structural changes to the organization and increases in flows of information. We chose this article because of its description of the growing need for visual displays as the world becomes more complex.

On Visualizing Quantitative Data

Tufte, E. R. (1997). *Visual and statistical thinking: Displays of evidence for making decisions*. Graphics Press.

This is a reprint of a chapter from a larger book by Tufte. In this chapter, Tufte relates two historical examples of how the visualization of quantitative data was used (or misused) and the resultant consequences. We chose this monograph to highlight the importance of visualizing data—whether quantitative or qualitative—and the importance of how those data are portrayed.

On Using Computer Coding to Create System Models

Wilensky, U., & Rand, W. (2015). *An introduction to agent-based modeling: Modeling natural, social, and engineered complex systems with NetLogo*. The MIT Press.

This book describes agent-based modeling and how to use it to understand better systems of all kinds. Depicting a system may also mean using methods that are outside the scope of this book, such as agent-based modeling. We chose this book because using agent-based modeling and computer coding to create depictions is another way to help people make their assumptions visible and to see the consequential patterns as they occur at the system level.

References

Banathy, B. H. (1995). Developing a systems view of education. *Educational Technology, 35*(3), 53–57. www.jstor.org/stable/44428279

Beer, S. (2002). What is cybernetics? *Kybernetes, 31*(2), 209–219. https://doi.org/10.1108/03684920210417283

Boardman, J., & Sauser, B. (2013). *Systemic thinking: Building maps for worlds of systems*. John Wiley & Sons.

Bohr, N. (1928). The quantum postulate and the recent development of atomic theory. *Nature, 121*(3050), 580–590. https://doi.org/10.1038/121580a0

Buchanan, R. (1992). Wicked problems in design thinking. *Design Issues, 8*(2), 5–21. https://doi.org/10.2307/1511637

Checkland, P. (1999). *Systems thinking, systems practice: Includes a 30-year retrospective*. John Wiley & Sons.

Checkland, P., & Poulter, J. (2020). Soft Systems Methodology. In M. Reynolds & S. Holwell (Eds.), *Systems approaches to making change: A practical guide* (pp. 201–253). Springer. https://doi.org/10.1007/978-1-4471-7472-1_5

Churchman, C. W. (1971). *The design of inquiring systems: Basic concepts of systems and organization*. Basic Books.

Collins, J. (2005). *Good to great and the social sectors: A monograph to accompany good to great*. Harper Business.

Forrester, J. W. (2007). System dynamics—A personal view of the first fifty years. *System Dynamics Review, 23*(2–3), 345–358. https://doi.org/10.1002/sdr.382

Gharajedaghi, J. (2011). *Systems thinking: Managing chaos and complexity: A platform for designing business architecture* (3rd ed.). Morgan Kaufmann.

Gorod, A., Hallo, L., & Merchant, S. (2021). Governance of patient-centered care: A systemic approach to cancer treatment. *Systems Research and Behavioral Science, 38*(2), 257–271. https://doi.org/10.1002/sres.2728

Khansari, N., Finger, M. Mostashari, A., & Mansouri, M. (2016). Conceptual systemigram model: Impact of electronic governance on sustainable development. *International Journal of System of Systems Engineering, 7*(4), 258–276. https://doi.org/10.1504/IJSSE.2016.080317

Nelson, H. G., & Stolterman, E. (2014). *The design way: Intentional change in an unpredictable world*. The MIT Press.

Regenold, T. A. (2020). *Local workforce development, federally legislated purposes, and a systemigram: A mixed-methods study* (Publication No. 28089820) [Doctoral dissertation, Old Dominion University]. ProQuest Dissertations and Theses Global.

Regenold, T. A., & Reed, P. A. (2023, March 23). Strategic planning and systemigrams: A mixed-methods study of the public system of workforce development. *Performance Improvement Quarterly*. https://doi.org/10.56811/PIQ-22-0028

Sauser, B., Mansouri, M., & Omer, M. (2011). Using systemigrams in problem definition: A case study in maritime resilience for Homeland Security. *Journal of Homeland Security and Emergency Management, 8*(1). https://doi.org/10.2202/1547-7355.1773

Smuts, J. C. (1927). *Holism and evolution* (2nd ed.). Macmillan and CO. https://archive.org/details/holismandevoluti032439mbp/page/n7/mode/2up

Systems Engineering Research Center. (n.d.). *Tools: SystemiTool*. [Software]. https://sercuarc.org/serc-tools/

Chapter 3

Evaluating the System

Systemic evaluation provides a lens through which you, as a public manager, can see the social system in its entirety. As a practice, evaluating the system ensures the health and viability of the organization as a whole. Included in the word "evaluation" is the root word "value." As a public manager, you have the opportunity to communicate that employees are valued and bring value to the system of which they are a part.

Evaluation of public sector organizations typically begins with program evaluation. Program evaluation as a practice involves framing questions prior to implementing an initiative, planning what data are to be gathered, collecting data, analyzing data, and communicating findings answering the question: "Was it worth it?" Historically, program evaluation, including formative and summative evaluation, has served a necessary and useful function for organizations.

One primary function of program evaluation is in supporting decision analysis (Fitzpatrick et al., 2011; Stufflebeam, 1968). Ultimately, the value of program evaluation is in its facilitation of results associated with improved services and quality of life (Madaus & Stufflebeam, 2000; Martin, 2015). The dynamic nature of program and service delivery supports the need for handling evaluation in a rigorous and flexible way (Martin, 2015). Effective program evaluation includes frequent and in-depth communication between evaluators and you as a public manager.

While program evaluation brings considerable value to individual initiatives and programs, it should be noted that program evaluation has often been employed primarily as a vehicle for securing or retaining funding from outside sources (Guba & Stufflebeam, 1970). Secondly, program evaluation historically focuses on a specific initiative or program rather than on the organizational system as a whole. Thirdly, program evaluation is generally performed by an individual or a team separate from the managers and staff who deliver the services. In the best case of program evaluation, the evaluators and the program staff confer regularly and frequently

DOI: 10.4324/9781003335153-3

to ensure benefits from formative evaluation and jointly aim at the delivery of effective results from summative evaluation.

Despite the obvious value of this practice, we submit that a more centrally established, integral, and inclusive form of systemic evaluation positions the organization to deliver optimum value for the people you serve. Evaluation integrates hard data and soft data to demonstrate outcomes and impact, including effects on knowledge, behavior, and attitudes, as well as economic and social change. The focus of systemic evaluation must be on the stability of the organization to deliver services consistently and responsively in a dynamic environment. A viable organizational system supported and developed by continuous systemic evaluation is an investment in service quality, consistency, and dependability (Murphy & Regenold, 2023). Ultimately, the stability of an organizational system has a profound impact on service quality and social change. But how can you as a public manager evaluate an entire system while still paying attention to the individual needs of employees and the people you serve?

About the Practice

Evaluating the system represents an opportunity for public managers to guide the organization toward becoming a responsive system. Starting with the purpose and continually gathering intelligence from the environment that surrounds the organizational system, you as a public manager set the stage for discovering and building linkages among parts of the system. Ongoing formative feedback informs you as a public manager of the system's capacity for responding to the authorizing purpose and thereby fulfilling the needs of customers. Summative evaluation utilizes formative feedback to achieve results. The complementary concept of continuous process improvement supports system refinement through a regular review and upgrade of processes that support the organizational system.

The Viable System Model

Ensuring the health and viability of the whole system is the point of systemic evaluation. The Viable System Model (VSM) developed by Beer (1972) provides a framework through which to evaluate a social organization systemically in terms of functions and interactions. Six interactive functions are emphasized in the VSM. These include productivity, coordination, operations, audit, development, and identity (Beer, 1972, 1984, 2007; Ramírez-Gutiérrez et al., 2021; Schwaninger & Scheef, 2016). Viability means the ability of a system to withstand disturbances from the environment and maintain its ability to function. A viable system resembles a sturdy building designed to remain intact when facing earthquakes or high winds.

In a viable system, the six functions work in harmony with one another, making the system better equipped to withstand the fluctuations, disturbances, and environmental chaos coming to the organization. One of the tenets of the VSM is that the organization must maintain sufficient variety, of ideas and actions available, to match or exceed the variety found in the outer environment (Fitch et al., 2014). Ideally, the organizational system must be poised to increase internal variety through diversity, equity, inclusion, and accessibility, for example.

Authorizing legislation defines the purpose or mission of a public social system, and the social system continually interacts with the political, economic, and social environments in which the organization operates. The six functions of the Viable System Model mutually interact to establish a continually improved capacity to deliver value that ultimately transforms the environment. The Viable System Model for Social Systems is displayed in Figure 3.1.

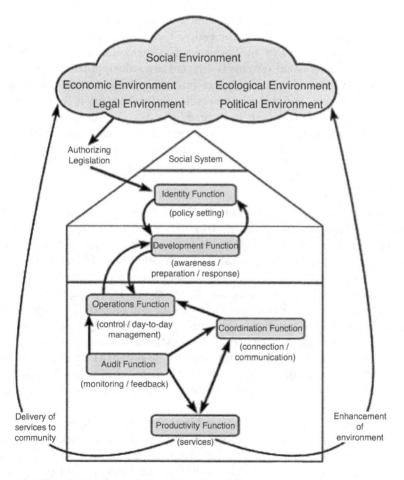

Figure 3.1 The Viable System Model for Social Systems.

Source: Adapted from Beer (1984)

The Productivity Function

The productivity function defines the services the system delivers. Specifically, these are the services the organization delivers daily; the services that the community recognizes as what the organization exists to provide. The productivity function is the primary work of the organization; it is what the frontline staff are working on each day.

As an example, outreach services for youth experiencing homelessness are intended to keep youth safe and move them to stable housing. An important facet of outreach services is helping youth build healthy relationships with caring adults. Outreach services exemplify the productivity function by recognizing the needs and delivering the primary social services on which people depend.

The productivity function benefits from systemic evaluation that provides current information about what is being delivered, how it is being experienced and perceived by the people receiving programs and services, as well as how programs and services affect the community. The productivity function in social systems is directed toward supporting people who receive services to integrate change into their lives, sustain the positive effects of services, and gain greater resilience. Productivity is the function in which employees' value can most readily be acknowledged—individually and as a team, department, or organization. It is also the function in which clients' views should be heard, recognized, and integrated.

The Coordination Function

The Coordination function connects the parts of the system through proactive and continuous communication. Designing and adjusting the flow of information to people responsible for parts of the system influence the productivity function by ensuring internal connectivity and supporting the value employees bring. The coordination function ensures that all parts of the system connect to serve clients effectively. Delivering effective services depends on your communicating to the community the range of services available. Also important is ensuring that you as a public manager in charge of a specific service area generate staff awareness of other related services and how staff efforts contribute to the system as a whole. Systemic evaluation of the coordination function benefits the system by ensuring awareness and connectivity among staff and stakeholders who provide services to clients.

For example, cities providing neighborhood services support clean, safe neighborhoods. Safe neighborhoods require engaging residents in actively monitoring the physical space, investing in cleanliness and safety, and reporting service needs to the city. Neighborhood-based facilities that provide meals, social support, and mental health services may be included.

Through ongoing systemic evaluation, a big picture understanding of how the components of neighborhood services relate to one another enriches the results. The coordination function supports the effectiveness of such services by identifying valued resources (e.g., human, fiscal, technological) and facilitating stakeholders' awareness through proactive communication and distribution. Ultimately, coordination supports a fluid and engaged organizational system that serves the community effectively.

The Operations Function

The operations function of the Viable System Model focuses on how services are delivered and what resources are required for improved performance. The operations function focuses on the control and effective operation of the organizational system to guide resources most efficiently and effectively to serve clients' needs and provide a healthy working environment for employees. Systemically evaluating the system through the lens of the operation function provides a means of responding to constant shifts in the operating environment as well as internal changes in productivity made clear through the coordination function.

For example, state-level services to support individuals with developmental disabilities are designed to help individuals lead healthy lives and pursue meaningful activities. The operations function entails the organization and orchestration of multiple facets of service delivery in such areas as healthcare, education, and other social services. Evaluating the operations function may mean identifying effective and efficient processes and working to improve them continuously, ensuring their connection with the system's purposes.

The operations function confirms clear, organized, well-orchestrated services delivered in a reliable and responsive way. The operations function ensures control of systemic service delivery in a holistic sense. Control of the system's performance necessitates sufficient internal variety of ideas and actions to match those found in the outer environment (Ashby, 1999). You as a public manager should also be mindful of the constraint of suboptimization. Suboptimization means that a part of the system is optimized at the expense of the whole system (Schwaninger & Scheef, 2016). Suboptimization is a competitive expression of organizational life. It is also a way of stating that one part of the system is not paying attention to the whole. For the system to operate viably, no single part of the system can be allowed to overtake the larger purpose.

The Audit Function

The audit function as defined by Beer (1972, 1984, 2007) monitors both vertical and lateral dimensions of operations. Monitoring performance on a regular basis ensures the accurate transfer of information vertically to senior management and to all levels of staff, in addition to laterally across departments or divisions and with provider partner organizations. The audit function informs the system by observing service, collecting data, and communicating information about service delivery via the operations function.

Feedback relevant to the current service status is supplied through the audit function. The audit function provides evidence of both positive service provision and areas needing improvement. Auditing is more narrowly focused on the numbers and the facts of service, while evaluation is broader. The audit function supports advocacy for clients by providing oversight. Acknowledging employees who perform the audit function as client advocates is one way to demonstrate their value to the organizational system.

An example of the importance of the auditing function in social services can be found in the area of public health in city government. Communicating information about threats to health and preventive measures available to residents, as well as conveying progress on metrics associated with health conditions, is vital to operations. Your tracking of keeping the public "in the know" about the status of infectious diseases and the measures that individuals and families can take to protect themselves and their communities is an example of how the audit function contributes to systemic evaluation.

Evaluating the audit function systemically requires proactivity in identifying which data should be collected. The benefits of systemic evaluation of the audit function include emphasis on meeting client needs effectively while remaining open to emerging needs within a changing environment. In the instance of public health in city government, the audit function specifies relevant statistics that can be published on a dashboard to ensure current knowledge for service providers, elected officials, public managers, and members of the public. The audit function means you continually collect and report current data and information that informs the operations function.

Ultimately, the audit function drives the productivity function and guides the operations function while providing client advocacy. Audit-based information is communicated as part of the coordination function, ensuring a balanced flow of information. The audit function is a vital and energizing function of the Viable System Model that contributes to systemic evaluation.

The Development Function

The development function emphasizes gaining intelligence from the outer environment (e.g., social, political, economic) for the purpose of crafting an adaptive response. The development function blends internal and external intelligence to define expectations for services to clients. Organizational relevance and responsiveness are key facets of the development function, emphasizing management and relationships throughout the system (Schwaninger, 2006) for the benefit of employees, clients, and other stakeholders. The ongoing collection of information about internal and external needs and the potential means of delivering services remains the focus of this important intelligence-gathering function.

An example of the development function can be found in the area of child welfare at the state level. Protecting children from abuse and neglect and supporting and sustaining healthy families requires considerable internal and external intelligence gained through the development function. Home visits to determine levels of safety and programs that guide healthy parenting comprise efforts by state agencies seeking to ensure child safety.

The development function represents an investment in data, information, and knowledge that guides the design of programs and services poised to eradicate threats to child safety. Maintaining currency about the impact of changing circumstances in the social environment supports clarity of purpose. Systemic evaluation of the development function informs the system of the most critical needs for services and paves the way for guiding delivery of relevant and effective services.

The Identity Function

The identity function represents the essence of the organization and provides direction and messaging to clients, employees, and the public about the organizational system. Stakeholders of the internal system and the general public alike look to the identity function to shape the direction via clear messaging about the organization as a system. The top leadership of the organization typically fulfills the identity function as it represents the system to wider spheres and guides conformance with and the development of policies. Further, the identity function is the ultimate decision-making entity of the organization (Ramírez-Gutiérrez et al., 2021).

Three facets of balance are focal for the identity function. The first facet involves balancing the internal organization and its workings with the outer environment (Ramírez-Gutiérrez et al., 2021; Schwaninger & Scheef, 2016). The second involves balancing current and anticipated needs. Thirdly, and importantly, the identity function must balance the reason for being of the organization, both within and outside the organization (Schwaninger & Scheef, 2016), in the context of the broader system of government, community, and society. This third function provides you as a public manager a focused opportunity to bring stakeholders of the system together in understanding and acting upon the organization's purposes.

An example of the identity function can be found in the chief local elected officials and the city manager of a municipality. For internal staff, clients, other stakeholders, and the general public in a local area, the elected officials and the city manager represent "the face" of this organization. The identity function represents the messaging vehicle and the responsible entity that sets policy and "steers the ship" toward productive and valuable performance. Proactively communicating with the community about internal initiatives, actively seeking new input from the environment, and integrating the two around the system purpose is the job of top leadership.

Systemic evaluation of the identity function benefits the social system by ensuring that clear messaging about the system purpose and services balances public expectation and commitment of social system professionals. The identity function is made viable and sustainable by maintaining clear, frequent, relevant, and customized messaging both within the organization and to the external environment. Within the organization, you as a public manager benefit from briefing staff, clients, and other stakeholders on service delivery status and opportunities for improvement. In parallel, scheduled events for the public such as "state of the city" addresses should be established as an expectation and shared through media outlets. Regular systemwide communication maintains the viability of the identity function and facilitates its serving in concert with the other functions of the Viable System Model.

Conducting Systemic Evaluation Using the Six Functions

As a public manager, you are responsible for evaluating the system systemically, which means overseeing the evaluation of the entire system while paying attention to the individual needs of employees and clients. The human dimension of systemic evaluation cannot be overstated. Human service is best evaluated systemically by integrating the needs, discoveries, knowledge, and commitment of people (Murphy & Regenold, 2023). Demonstrating respect for the experience and viewpoints of clients, staff, and stakeholders is what makes public service a remarkable profession characterized by the recognition of human dignity and equality among individuals.

Integrating the valuing of people with the quantitative and qualitative assessment of service effectiveness systemwide is at the core of systemic evaluation (Vickers, 1983). Communicating directly to individuals, teams, and entire departments that we value them is vitally important. Likewise, clients need to hear the message that we respect them and what they share. Engaging with employees, stakeholders, and clients and providing positive feedback as well as working together to discover ways to improve what we do is inherent in systemic evaluation.

Systemic evaluation includes all six functions of the Viable System Model: Productivity, coordination, operations, audit, development, and identity (Beer, 1972, 1984, 2007; Ramírez-Gutiérrez et al., 2021; Schwaninger & Scheef, 2016). The six functions of the Viable System Model work together to ensure that you as a public manager are producing services that add value. Those services are coordinated through clear and frequent communication. You as a public manager commit to devoting the resources needed on a continual basis in response to social, economic, political, and other changes. You can further integrate the intelligence gained through the development function as relevant, worthy of understanding, and informing of your effort to serve. Finally, the identity function must offer an inspiring and generative message to staff and stakeholders about who you are as a system, why you exist, and what you are to do as you take on responsibilities that can make a difference in your communities.

Evaluating systemically involves continually discovering the individual needs of employees and clients through active listening, learning their perspectives, and acting upon new knowledge obtained through the framework of the six functions. The design and delivery of services should reflect needs as you learn about them from direct dialogue and input from people who serve and people who receive services. Systemic evaluation is richer than traditional evaluation. For example, the word "audit" is typically associated with finding mistakes and correcting them. Rather than checking the box associated with itemized lists of requirements, a deeper, more systemic approach to the audit function entails clearly expressing advocacy for clients. Likewise, developing strong and positive relationships with staff and stakeholders deepens the shared responsibility of evaluation. As a public manager, you energize individuals and teams to embrace what they know about the people we serve and act upon that knowledge.

Structuring systemic evaluation begins with identifying who is already responsible for performing each of these functions. Further, systemic evaluation necessitates regularly performed, reliable efforts to collect data and apply information and knowledge to guide future assessment and performance improvement. Gathering and sharing that information with clients, staff, and other stakeholders emphasizes the evolution of service design and delivery. Specifying responsibility for evaluating the system based on viability as defined by the six functions ensures an ongoing, systemwide commitment to assessing current service and continuously improving performance.

One way of conducting systemic evaluation is to establish a core evaluation team responsible for reviewing formative and summative evaluation information monthly, bimonthly, or quarterly. The evaluation team can include managers or supervisors and direct service providers within the organization and service provider partners. The team may report to a manager with oversight responsibility for service delivery and agree upon a level of frequency for reporting evaluation findings. An integral part of reporting should include dialogue about needs, services, and results of service delivery with all staff and stakeholders who have roles connected to the six functions.

Systemic evaluation should include formative and summative dimensions based on client and staff perceptions. Formative evaluation addresses the needs of employees and clients by asking them for their feedback and input about the effectiveness of the system. Summative evaluation considers the performance and impact of the system's functioning as a whole.

The Formative Feedback Loops Tool (Figure 3.2) illustrates a way to integrate the individual needs of employees and clients. For summative evaluation, the Systems Analysis Tool (Figure 3.3) provides specific questions pertinent to the six functions and can guide questions of viability, service delivery, and efficiency as well as outcomes reflecting community impact. Ultimately, systemic evaluation integrates current reality with new needs discovered through a fusion of qualitative human interaction and quantitative indicators (Vickers, 1983) of service effectiveness and community change.

Included in formative assessment in systemic evaluation are the following:

- Immediate feedback that can lead to small changes in programs, processes, and services.
- New perspectives regarding service opportunities based on client, staff, and stakeholder insights.
- Opportunities for changes in service design and quality based on changes in the environment (e.g., social, economic, and political).

Included in summative assessment in systemic evaluation are the following:

- Summary data regarding program and service impact at the logical end of a program cycle.
- Number of clients served during this period compared to the prior period correlated with changes in the environment (e.g., social, economic, and political).
- Impact of completed programs and services on the community.

Overall, valuing becomes the focal point of emphasis in systemic evaluation. You as a public manager can shape system viability by including individual stakeholders' interests in optimizing effectiveness. As a public manager, you are able to ensure that all system energy is directed toward valuing and evaluating to stimulate continuous improvement and guide the system toward consistent delivery of strong, positive, viable, and sustainable services.

Box 3.1   Theory Box: Evaluating the System.

A systemic thinking approach to evaluation encompasses the functions of a viable system as they support fulfillment of the organizational purpose. The practice of evaluating the system relies on consideration of the whole system, interest in how parts of the system connect and communicate, and a desire for the system to become more effective in serving clients. Relevant systems principles and aspects of systemic thinking are described below.

Systems Thinking Principles

Systems thinking principles were derived from original sources whenever possible. We used original sources to incorporate the history of systems thinking and to acknowledge the progenitors of the principles. The following systems thinking principles support the practice of evaluating the system:

- *The Law of Requisite Variety.* Ashby's (1999) Law of Requisite Variety indicates that for an organizational system to be autonomous as a system, it must have the internal variety, expressed as ideas and actions, to equal or exceed the complexity in the operating environment. Absent such variety, the system will not possess sufficient strength to withstand the external pressures of the environment. Should the organization succumb to external pressures, the environment alone will determine what the organization is able to produce (Ashby, 1999).
- *Dynamic Equilibrium.* The systems principle of dynamic equilibrium supports a perpetually evolving sense of order in the system. As forces in the environment are discovered through the development function, the internal system must maintain itself as a stable entity that can withstand ongoing change. While all social systems tend to approximate a sense of equilibrium, none will actually reach a perfectly calibrated state (Parsons, 1952). The system must invest in its ability to maintain itself to meet its service commitments.

- *System Learning.* A supporting systems principle for the audit function is system learning as proposed by Argyris (1991). Beginning with the identification of errors, both single loop learning (i.e., maintaining current system structure) and double loop learning (i.e., questioning assumptions, approaches, and culture) provide important evaluative insights that help members of the system learn ways to enhance the system over time (Argyris, 1991). Stakeholders of a social system must learn together on behalf of the system to optimize its effectiveness.

Critical Thinking Aspects

Evaluating the system benefits from critical thinking about the assumptions and logic that underlie how the organization designs and delivers services to fulfill its purposes. Applying critical thinking to systemic evaluation involves the following points:

- Explore what we as a system currently measure and how we measure it.
- Examine the effectiveness of current metrics and make changes as needed.
- Assess the level of fair-mindedness regarding service design and delivery.
- Determine the resources needed to sustain service.
- Examine the impact of services on individual lives and communities.

Design Thinking Aspects

Design thinking involves transforming ideas into reality. When evaluating the organizational system, you as a public manager employ design thinking as a creative means of acting upon critical thinking and systems thinking to invent a new approach to serving customers. You as a public manager are able to encourage design thinking by staff and stakeholders in reshaping the organization. To encourage design thinking:

- Use evaluative information to shape the system to do a better job of serving people and making lasting change.
- Look for system strengths during evaluations to support systemic resilience and impact communities.
- Recognize system shortcomings as opportunities for redesign.

Case Study: A Town Manager Faces Challenges With Evaluating Performance

A case study focused on evaluating the system is presented to illustrate two ways of approaching a situation. The first is a non-systemic, linear-analytical approach that employs a compartmentalized, competitive way of perceiving the challenge. The second is a systemic approach that reflects a comprehensive way of addressing the issue, including a linear-analytical approach. While traditional, linear thinking has merits, a holistic approach amplifies the potential for evaluating the system as a whole. Such systemic thinking stimulates the inclusive involvement of multiple system stakeholders in a comprehensive approach to evaluation.

Non-systemic Approach

A new town manager was appointed by the town council to take over the organization after a succession of previous managers was unable to deliver the results desired by elected officials. No town manager had been successful in guiding staff toward defining clear and important measures. A major factor in the decision to hire the new town manager was her indication that evaluating performance was something she was good at doing.

Two council members who were themselves business owners in the community consistently expressed a need to provide a dashboard showing real-time measures for tracking several areas of performance. These council members heard from fellow elected officials at conferences that dashboards provide transparency. Council members themselves disagreed as to the major metrics, but asserted during a discussion, "Give it to the staff; they'll figure it out."

In her zeal to get to work and demonstrate responsiveness, the new town manager assembled her staff and explained how important measurement was to the council. She hastily planned a two-day meeting of her top reports to decide what metrics to include in the dashboard and placed considerable emphasis on working with the Information Technology (IT) Department to determine how the dashboard would be displayed and how soon it could be put together. Staff and IT worked together during the two-day meeting. That meeting focused on three questions: (1) What metrics do we have now? (2) What does the council probably want for metrics? (3) How fast can we get this going, so the council will be satisfied?

Discussions that followed included a litany of examples of current metrics used by staff. The person who headed Human Resources (HR) shared that his department had been tracking results for years. Most of these metrics pertained to hiring staff, firing staff, and resignations. The town clerk voiced the view that her department had been tracking requests for documents and election registrations for a long time. These, she stated, would surely qualify for dashboard information. Water and sewer service staff shared that they collected information about calls requesting services and cases closed. Police and fire staff shared that they know how many crimes of various types occur, how many and what types of fires have been fought, and that they consistently track service calls. Those staff responsible for bringing in new business to the community stated that they can "rattle off" what new businesses are preparing to come to town, as well as the likely number of new jobs that will result.

The manager felt heartened by the number of elements currently being measured. She proposed to the staff that the various departments compete to have "the best measures" to add to the planned dashboard. The manager further proposed that competing departments could earn prizes, including paid time off, for departments winning the dashboard metrics competition.

As the town manager and department heads jockeyed to prepare a presentation to council, they concluded that the town truly "measures everything," and spoke enthusiastically about the competition to showcase metrics on a public-facing dashboard. The dashboard was seen as a way to "show off" how business-like the town was, and thereby encourage new business to come to the town.

Just as the management team was preparing to present the new dashboard to the council, an unforeseen event happened. One of the largest firms in town announced that it was leaving the community to relocate to an area with greater economic prospects. The council and the town manager were devastated by this news. As staff prepared to go to the council with its plans for the dashboard, members hoped that what they had to offer would make up for the disappointment the community felt in face of the reality of the city's losing business and jobs.

Systemic Approach

Following a series of attempts to hire a town manager who would stay in the position and shape organizational performance going forward, the town council appointed an individual with a track record of building both performance and unity among staff in her previous management positions in government. One of the primary points of interest the council had for a new manager was the ability to track and showcase progress toward strong service to members of the community.

The council and the town manager agreed that it was important to "read" the business community and the residents to ensure that the town functioned with full commitment to delivering service that was relevant and responsive to the town. The manager shared with the council a plan to bring together her direct reports, stakeholders, community and business leaders, and the council in a public meeting. The purpose of this meeting was to build and share knowledge about the functioning of the town as one holistic entity of responsive productivity. Three elements needed focus in the face-to-face session. First, inputs to build a common understanding; second, outputs, showing the results produced; and third, outcomes that provided evidence of impacts on the community.

During the first phase of the meeting, the town manager sought to build a common understanding of the purpose of the town organization and what it existed to deliver, according to state statute, the town charter, and the expectations of residents and businesses in the community. She posed questions about the needs of businesses and community members. The town manager emphasized that all viewpoints were relevant and important to gathering the best intelligence the town had available. Further, the organization needed to be clear about what resources it had, how performance was managed in evaluating the quality of services, and how well the parts of the organizational system connected and communicated. Also critical was the extent to which collaboration among staff, elected officials, and stakeholders was optimized to create the greatest value for those living in the town.

With these important inputs determined and defined for members of the system, the second phase of understanding pertained to outputs and outcomes delivered by the town. What did the town produce for the community? How did the town learn from its service delivery and the responses of residents over time? How did the town as an organization initiate and embrace change? What impact did the performance and activities of the town government have on people's lives, businesses, and the community?

The town manager emphasized several important facets of how the organization should consider the work of evaluating itself, learning from what was found, and making change as the outer environment presented shifts in the political, economic, and social environment. It was deemed important to let the community know with one voice that the town was there to support members of the community as the provider of services that ran well and continually improved in capability.

Council members and town staff alike agreed that it would be helpful to identify measures that could be shared on a regular basis with the community at large. They agreed that such an endeavor had value but required careful analysis, enriched by perspectives shared by many stakeholders, to ensure that the town did not provide an endless stream of meaningless metrics. Better, they determined, to focus on measures that emphasized impactful change in the community.

The town manager asked for participation in work groups to establish metrics that emphasized outputs and outcomes. These metrics would distil the information to help community members learn the number of people served by programs, the level of participation, and major change in the quality of life in such areas as public safety, revenues collected for utilities and services, and economic development for the community.

After rich discussions among stakeholders, staff, and elected officials, members of the town government agreed that the question, "How are we doing?" needed to be addressed continuously by all parties as one strong organization. Each facet of service would be reflected, including public safety, economic development, public utilities, and quality of life. Where there existed opportunities to strengthen service, it would be important to design policies, processes, and practices in a manner that would support ongoing learning and adaptation.

Tools

Two tools are provided in this chapter to support the practice of Evaluating the System:

1. Formative Feedback Loops Tool for supporting continuous progress that leads to summative results.
2. Systems Analysis Tool for rating multiple functions critical to the organization's performance.

These tools incorporate both formative and summative dimensions of evaluation and guide a systemic view of evaluating and improving social services. Meeting the needs of people who depend upon social services necessitates a clear examination of what is being done, how we learn to enrich current levels of service, and how we integrate dimensions of need and the potential for service improvement.

Formative Feedback Loops Tool

The Formative Feedback Loops tool provides employees, departments, and leaders a means of addressing two categories of healthy system functioning: (1) inputs and (2) outputs/outcomes. The tool employs a sequential flow of formative evaluation components. The sequence begins on the middle-left side of the tool, starting with (1) intelligence (e.g., about the political, social, and economic environments), and moving clockwise, to (2) resources, to (3) management, to (4) coordination, and finally to (5) collaboration as a primary method of structuring system-level value for the people served by the organization. Included with each component in the sequence is a question that the internal evaluation team should pose and address.

FORMATIVE FEEDBACK LOOPS TOOL

Formative Feedback is an informal process of information gathering and sharing between and among employees, departments, and leaders. **Formative Feedback Loops** are ongoing to support progress in a continuous way and ultimately lead to stronger summative results. Items 1-5 describe Inputs. Items 6-9 describe Outputs and Outcomes.

Instructions: Beginning with Item #1, Intelligence, ask each question of individual employees, supervisors, managers, and/or leaders. Take notes on their responses. To obtain a formative assessment of your system, review your notes as a collection and identify themes or trends from the responses.

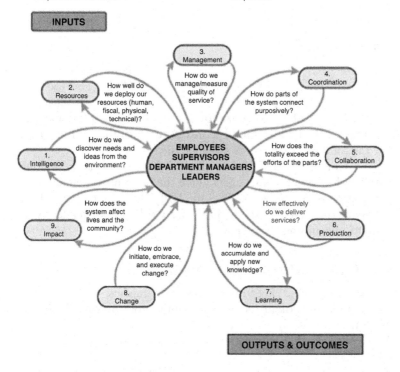

Figure 3.2 Formative Feedback Loops Tool.

For outputs/outcomes, the sequence begins at the middle right side of the tool and proceeds in a clockwise flow starting with (6) production, and proceeding to (7) learning, to (8) change, and to (9) impact. Included with each component in the output/outcome category is a question pertaining to service delivery, investment in the organizational system to create yet more value, and finally leading to change and impact on the community served by the organization. See Figure 3.2.

Other Potential Uses of the Formative Feedback Loops Tool

- As a guide for examining a particular input (intelligence, resources, etc.) that has current relevance based on an environmental condition.
- As an educational tool to share inputs and outputs with new employees, potential system partners, and existing stakeholders.
- As an exploratory tool for identifying areas of emphasis for systemic thinking about the long-term impact of the system.
- As a vehicle for identifying potential resources to support new social service needs in the system.

Systems Analysis Tool

The Systems Analysis Tool is based on the six functions established in the Viable System Model (VSM) developed by Beer (1972). This tool includes several evaluative statements for each of the functions introduced in this chapter. Members of the organizational system rate each statement within each category, then add subtotal scores for each of the six functions. The higher the total score, the more systemic the organization.

The Systems Analysis Tool furnishes a basis for discussion among system stakeholders. Public managers guide the ongoing systemic evaluation by using the Systems Analysis Tool to clarify the degree to which the six functions of the Viable System Model are working independently and in relation to one another. See Figure 3.3.

Other Potential Uses of the Systems Analysis Tool

- As a tool for identifying future needs in operations.
- As an indicator of areas of opportunity for improving community impact.
- As a vehicle for designing systemic communication to support system identity.
- As a means of supporting learning from the environment.

Chapter Summary

Evaluation is central to the way an organization is managed. Systemic evaluation provides the lens through which to see the social system in its entirety. The practice of systemic evaluation provides a rich opportunity to broaden and deepen knowledge by you as a public manager and by staff, stakeholders, and elected officials who are part of the organizational system. Ongoing formative feedback including both quantitative and qualitative information informs you as a public manager of the system's capacity

SYSTEMS ANALYSIS TOOL

Systems Analysis is a form of evaluation that examines an organizational system's primary functions and relationships holistically, typically at the end of an evaluation period.

Instructions: Rate items 1 - 20 (1 = lowest, 5 = highest). Subtotal each function's score (e.g., productivity, coordination, etc.). Finally, add the subtotals and fill in the total score.

Function	Statement	Rating Scale (1 = lowest, 5 = highest)	Rating
	1. We deliver services efficiently.	1 2 3 4 5	
	2. We deliver services effectively.	1 2 3 4 5	
	3. The system positively affects employees.	1 2 3 4 5	
	4. The system positively affects those it serves.	1 2 3 4 5	
Productivity	5. The system positively affects the community in which it is located.	1 2 3 4 5	
		Productivity Subtotal	**/25**
	6. Parts of the system connect purposively.	1 2 3 4 5	
Coordination	7. Coordination supports productivity in our system.	1 2 3 4 5	
		Coordination Subtotal	**/10**
	8. Management decisions address current needs.	1 2 3 4 5	
	9. Management anticipates future needs.	1 2 3 4 5	
Operations	10. Management decisions address future needs.	1 2 3 4 5	
		Operations Subtotal	**/15**
	11. We measure quality effectively.	1 2 3 4 5	
	12. We measure service effectively.	1 2 3 4 5	
Audit	13. Our services result in the realization of our mission.	1 2 3 4 5	
		Audit Subtotal	**/15**
	14. We study the environment (e.g., social, economic, etc.).	1 2 3 4 5	
	15. We learn from the environment.	1 2 3 4 5	
Development	16. We contribute to the environment in a positive way.	1 2 3 4 5	
		Development Subtotal	**/15**
	17. Customers clearly understand who we are as a system.	1 2 3 4 5	
	18. Stakeholders clearly understand who we are as a system.	1 2 3 4 5	
	19. Employees clearly understand who we are as a system.	1 2 3 4 5	
Identity	20. Our identity as a system evolves.	1 2 3 4 5	
		Identity Subtotal	**/20**
		Total	**/100**

Figure 3.3 Systems Analysis Tool.
Source: Adapted from Beer (1972)

for responding to the authorizing purpose(s) and delivering results that fulfill the needs of customers.

Two tools are included in this chapter to guide formative and summative evaluation, respectively. The Formative Feedback Loops Tool guides information gathering and sharing among key stakeholders of the system, integrating inputs, outputs, and outcomes in a cyclical pattern. The Viable System Model (VSM) developed by Beer (1972) provides a basis on which the summative evaluation tool, the Systems Analysis Tool, was developed, highlighting six key functions and their interactions that clarify current and potential performance.

Practicing the Practice

Several suggestions are provided to help you expand the practice of evaluating the system. As a public manager, you perform the role of facilitator in developing a common understanding of the purpose of systemic evaluation among staff and system partners. Likewise, your role involves communicating to staff and stakeholders effective ways of understanding how systemic evaluation supports productivity, service effectiveness, and improvement. In addition, your involving stakeholders in how to conduct ongoing evaluation of services is relevant to your role as a public manager. Practice supports the development of these roles.

Exploring Approaches to Evaluating the System
(See Case Study)

It is useful for you as a public manager to involve staff and stakeholders in designing evaluation of the system's performance. Creating meaningful approaches to measuring service delivery guides the organization's effectiveness in responding to service needs of the community. Your engaging staff in reviewing the case studies provides practice in shifting perspectives about approaches to measurement through systems thinking, critical thinking, and design thinking to ensure a strong and resilient system.

1. Review the Non-systemic Approach in the Case Study section during a meeting and pose these questions:

   a. What are some of the potential benefits and drawbacks of the non-systemic approach to evaluating the system?
   b. How would you describe the way staff, clients, and other stakeholders might have reacted to the town manager's use of metrics for evaluating the system?
   c. What might you do differently to ensure the development of meaningful approaches to measuring performance?

2. Request that meeting participants read the Systemic Approach in the Case Study section, and pose the following questions:

   a. What are some of the potential benefits and drawbacks of the systemic approach to evaluating the system?

   b. How would you describe the way staff, clients, and other stakeholders might have reacted to the town manager's approach to evaluating the system?

   c. What about the systemic approach used by the town manager would benefit our own organization?

Establishing Common Understanding of Systemic Evaluation (See Figure 3.2)

The Formative Feedback Loops Tool provides a way of understanding the inputs and outputs/outcomes pertinent to the organization's service delivery. Further, the tool affords each person an opportunity to recognize the ways that his or her role contributes to strengthening and sustaining the system to deliver value for the people served. You as a public manager facilitate shared understanding of how the contributions of each person and department can be brought together to transform inputs into outputs/outcomes that strengthen and sustain the system to deliver services.

1. Share the Formative Feedback Loops Tool with a group of staff and stakeholders.
2. Divide the group into two teams: Inputs Team and Outputs/Outcomes Team.
3. Ask the Inputs Team to explore the questions included on the tool for each of the areas noted on the Tool (Example: for the intelligence category, "How do we discover needs and ideas from the environment?").
4. Ask the Outputs/Outcomes Team to explore the questions included in the tool for each of the areas noted on the tool (Example: for the production category, "How effectively do we deliver services?").
5. Bring both teams back to the large group, and have each team brief the group on its discussion and key findings.
6. Ask all participants to share their reflections about the use of the Formative Feedback Loops Tool for evaluating your system.

Applying Systemic Evaluation (See Figure 3.3)

The Systems Analysis Tool provides summative evaluation measures that represent the effectiveness of systemic evaluation for the organization. For each function, there are two to five questions that can be used to clarify each function. It is valuable to assess the organization by involving staff and stakeholders in scoring each statement of the tool.

1. Gather a group of staff and stakeholders.
2. Ask each group to rate each of the items in the tool (1 = low; 5 = high).
3. Ask each group to share the sub-totaled score within each of the six categories.
4. Examine together the sub-scores for each category. Explore how the organization could improve its performance in each category.
5. Total the scores for all categories. (The higher the score, the more viable, vibrant, and systemic the organization.)
6. Discuss with the group what the organization needs to do to ensure future, ongoing results that support and sustain a viable and vibrant system.

Reflecting on Practicing the Practice

Reflection on the practice of evaluating the system promotes discernment and awareness. Thinking about, writing about, and discussing the chapter, using the tools, and practicing the practice allows you to consider ways to integrate systemic evaluation to stimulate and sustain positive change. Reflecting can take place as an individual or group activity. Consider the following questions and write or discuss your responses:

1. What worked about the practice of evaluating the system?
2. What did not work about the practice?
3. What did you notice about your own thinking during the practice?
4. What did you notice about the interactions and behaviors of others?
5. What changes in perspective about evaluating the system occurred as a result of practicing this practice?
6. What might you do differently the next time you practice this practice?

Recommended Readings

On the History of Evaluation

Hogan, R. L. (2007). The historical development of program evaluation: Exploring past and present. *Online Journal for Workforce Education and Development, 2*(4), Article 5. https://opensiuc.lib.siu.edu/ojwed/vol2/iss4/5

The field of evaluation has transitioned from a primarily summative emphasis to a fusion of formative and summative evaluation spanning the public and private sectors. We chose this article because it offers context for the reader seeking to understand how evaluation as a discipline has evolved over time.

On Theories and Models of Evaluation

Frye, A. W., & Hemmer, P. A. (2012). Program evaluation models and related theories: AMEE Guide No. 67. *Medical Teacher, 34*(5), e288–e299. https://doi.org/1 0.3109/0142159X.2012.668637

This article acknowledges the importance of change and the need for measuring change. The authors provide an informative summary of theories of evaluation, including reductionism, systems theory, and complexity theory. In addition, the article provides a range of evaluation models for application. We chose this article to acquaint the reader with theories and models that support evaluation.

On Systemic Evaluation

Reynolds, M., Gates, E., Hummelbrunner, R., Marra, M., & Williams, B. (2016). Towards systemic evaluation. *Systems Research and Behavioral Science, 33*(5), 662–673. https://doi.org/10.1002/sres.2423

This article explores ideas of systems thinking and complexity science (STCS) in contrast to institutionalized evaluation, which is more linear. Three ways of approaching systemic evaluation are proposed and discussed: (1) Connecting evaluations with a changing and fluid reality; (2) developing the ability to respond with empathy when evaluating; and (3) using adaptive STCS tools as part of evaluation practice. We chose this article for its emphasis on evaluation relevant to organizational systems.

References

Argyris, C. (1991). Teaching smart people how to learn. *Harvard Business Review*, 4(2). https://hbr.org/1991/05/teaching-smart-people-how-to-learn

Ashby, W. R. (1999). *An Introduction to cybernetics*. Chapman & Hall. http://pcp. vub.ac.be/books/IntroCyb.pdf (Original work published 1957).

Beer, S. (1972). *Brain of the firm: The managerial cybernetics of organization*. The Professional Library.

Beer, S. (1984). The Viable System Model: Its provenance, development, methodology and pathology. *Journal of the Operational Research Society, 35*(1), 7–25. https://doi.org/10.1057/jors.1984.2

Beer. S. (2007). *Diagnosing the system for organizations*. John Wiley & Sons.

Fitch, D., Parker-Barua, L., & Watt, J. W. (2014). Envisioning public child welfare agencies as learning organizations: Applying Beer's Viable System Model to Title IV-E program evaluation. *Journal of Public Child Welfare, 8*(2), 119–142. https://doi.org/10.1080/15548732.2013.879089

Fitzpatrick, J. L., Sanders, J. R., & Worthen, B. R. (2011). *Program evaluation: Alternative approaches and practical guidelines* (4th ed.). Pearson.

Guba, E.G., & Stufflebeam, D. L. (1970). *Evaluation: The process of stimulating, aiding, and abetting insightful action* (ED055733). ERIC. https://files.eric. ed.gov/fulltext/ED055733.pdf

Madaus, G. F., & Stufflebeam, D. L. (2000). Program evaluation: A historical overview. In D. L. Stufflebeam, G. F. Madaus & T. Kellaghan (Eds.), *Evaluation models: Viewpoints on educational and human services evaluation* (pp. 3–18). Springer. https://doi.org/10.1007/0-306-47559-6_1

Martin, A. B. (2015). Plan for program evaluation from the start. *National Institute of Justice Journal, 275,* 24–28. https://nij.ojp.gov/topics/articles/plan-program-evaluation-start

Murphy, S. E., & Regenold, T. A. (2023). Applying the Viable System Model to local government in a post-pandemic context. In E. Azukas & M. Kim (Eds.), *Reimagining systems thinking in a post-pandemic world* (pp. 79–96). IGI Global. https://doi.org/10.4018/978-1-6684-7285-9.ch004

Parsons, T. (1952). *The social system.* Tavistock Publications.

Ramírez-Gutiérrez, A. G., Cardoso-Castro, P. P., & Tejeida-Padilla, R. (2021). A methodological proposal for the complementarity of the SSM and the VSM for the analysis of viability in organizations. *Systemic Practice and Action Research, 34*(3), 331–357. https://doi.org/10.1007/s11213-020-09536-7

Schwaninger, M. (2006). Design for viable organizations: The diagnostic power of the viable system model. *Kybernetes, 35*(7–8), 955–966. https://doi.org/10.1108/03684920610675012

Schwaninger, M., & Scheef, C. (2016). A test of the Viable System Model: Theoretical claim vs. empirical evidence. *Cybernetics and Systems, 47*(7), 544–569. http://dx.doi.org/10.1080/01969722.2016.1209375

Stufflebeam, D. L. (1968). *Evaluation as enlightenment for decision making* (ED048333). ERIC. https://files.eric.ed.gov/fulltext/ED048333.pdf

Vickers, G. (1983). *Human systems are different.* Harper & Row.

Chapter 4

Collaborating Within and Across Systems

Collaborating within and across systems means engaging with other individuals, departments, or organizations to connect parts of the system to realize the system's purposes. The practice of collaboration expresses an important facet of systemic thinking in which you as a public manager guide the delivery of services that integrate multiple points of view, reflect the diverse needs of clients, and apply an array of resources to meet those needs. Social partnerships are dynamic and distinctly positioned to handle persistent challenges at different levels of complexity (Waddock, 1991).

Collaboration is a fundamentally interpersonal process supported by organizational and systemic factors (San Martín Rodríguez et al., 2005). Whether collaboration occurs within the system (i.e., between individuals, teams, or departments) or across systems with partner organizations (i.e., a multi-sector collaboration), the practice holistically broadens and deepens our understanding of sustainable social systems. In other words, collaboration is an essential building block for creating a vibrant, sustainable organization.

However, given mandates to collaborate, you as a public manager may feel pressured to engage in collaboration to obtain something in the short term: More funds, more clients, or a better reputation. An example involves a public organization that may agree to participate in a grant initiative spearheaded by a potential partner. The immediate purpose of taking part in the collaboration may be to gain revenue while simultaneously being seen as cooperative by other organizations. In this situation, you may feel an initial reluctance to participate due to what seems to be an absence of authentic collaboration. Systemic collaboration is one in which all partners are meaningfully included in shaping how the initiative will enhance the common purposes of the collaboration.

A different type of mandate may occur when your organization and another organization are known to have a common purpose and serve the

DOI: 10.4324/9781003335153-4

same clientele. For example, services provided to vulnerable populations within a given state may be mandated to work together in service delivery (Sandfort, 1999). Although the two organizations share the same clientele, the organizations may have different cultures, norms, and beliefs about the nature of their work and their clients' needs. One organization may have a negative perception of the other organization with which they are expected to collaborate. There may be mutual disdain or perceptions by one organization of the insufficiency of the other organization. A persistent refusal to work together may prompt a tacit rejection of the idea of collaboration that funders require.

In contrast, collaboration based on mutual commitment to shared goals provides a valuable foundation for engaging in the practice of systemic collaboration. A belief in the importance of serving a particular population stimulates the hard work of structuring collaboration. Engaging in thoughtful dialogue and developing ways to work together supports arranging complementary contributions and designing shared resources, structures, roles, and results. Such engagement paves the way for sustainable collaboration that builds the system and enhances its services. Given the typical constraints placed on collaboration, how can you as a public manager recognize, model, and guide collaborative efforts to make a difference in the quality of social system services for all involved?

About the Practice

Mandates to collaborate are nearly universal in government service and nonprofit work. Although increasing funding for organizations remains one reason to collaborate, other rationales for doing so include achieving efficiencies (Sowa, 2009), broadening ideas and perspectives of service professionals (Aiken & Hage, 1968), expanding expertise and breadth of knowledge (Flanigan, 2023), and effecting systemic change (Clarke & Crane, 2018). In other words, collaboration is one vehicle for inventing a new systemic reality.

Additional Obstacles to Collaborating

In addition to the situations mentioned earlier, rigid adherence to a long-term organizational purpose may interfere with a more flexible use of resources (Flanigan, 2023). For example, a nonprofit organization providing support to discourage justice-involved youth from using alcohol, tobacco, and other drugs may learn from the literature, best practices, and the environment that educating the family may contribute to the organization's purpose. Despite a legacy of narrower focus on the youth themselves, broadening the use of resources to support and sustain healthy families may be useful.

In other instances, organizations that have been directed to collaborate based on similar missions and service populations may face cultural and interpersonal conflict (Sandfort, 1999) despite what might appear to be a logical and productive arrangement of resources. As an example, a government agency and a nonprofit organization working with clients on social services in Michigan were required to collaborate. The rationale behind the mandate to collaborate was clear: The two organizations served the same population. Despite this, the cultures and beliefs of the two organizations differed substantially. One organization operated as a closed system, trusting only its own employees while perceiving the other organization as ineffective. In addition, messages to clients differed in style and substance and caused confusion among people the organizations were meant to serve (Sandfort, 1999).

An additionally persistent issue in the public sector is a pattern of demanding workloads for professionals. Within bureaucracies, heavy meeting schedules, low staffing levels, and requirements for extensive documentation may burden public managers and staff. Often in contention is the issue of what constitutes "real work" versus additional responsibilities that may be seen as less relevant. For individuals burdened by too many responsibilities and too little support, collaboration may be seen as doing "work on top of work" that is already too demanding. Despite suspicions to the contrary, the paradox of systemic collaboration is that investing the time ultimately can result in a reduced workload for participating professionals.

Another obstacle involves limiting collaboration to a few staff members in an interorganizational endeavor. In such instances, collaboration becomes person-dependent rather than organization-embraced. Limiting collaborative partnerships to selected individuals from a given organization rather than focusing collaboration on the broader organization detracts from its effectiveness. Systemic collaboration necessitates an authentic investment of commitment and resources at the organizational level rather than depending exclusively on specific individuals. The individual-centered approach places collaboration at risk when a given person leaves the organization. In such instances, the collaboration may be reduced in effectiveness or disappear altogether.

An additional issue involves non-responsive potential collaborators who sign on for a collaboration, then fail to respond in a timely way or ignore outreach and questions from other partners during the initiative. Collaboration is a multi-party endeavor, requiring that partners remain alert to the shared endeavor and communicate with others included in the system. Reciprocity in communication and task performance energizes collaboration. Absent such reciprocity, intended collaboration can be reduced to what amounts to a solo performance with reluctant partners who fail to show up consistently. The role of public managers is to engage in proactive communication, both in groups and in one-on-one conversations, to support and encourage shared projects and initiatives.

Managing Systemic Collaboration

Despite all these obstacles, managing systemic collaboration contributes to building a vibrant organizational system. A strong, well-coordinated system based on collaboration is made possible by the public manager, who engages in four key responsibilities:

- Shaping Resources.
- Supporting Structures.
- Clarifying Roles.
- Delivering Results.

Shaping Resources

When faced with the obstacle of organizations with different cultures who do not want to work together, you as a public manager can use shaping resources as a first step toward breaking down the walls between people. Redirecting attention away from interpersonal conflict and toward blending and shaping resources positions the collaborative for effectiveness. One point of collaboration is to elevate and encourage partners who share common purposes to design increasingly creative and effective ways to serve. The potential base of expanded resources sets the stage for working together using practical and rewarding approaches. Engaging in thoughtful dialogue about what the organizations are trying to do and how to improve that effort across systems emphasizes the application and shaping of capabilities, money, ideas, and creativity in a way that can change the lives of clients and communities.

As an example, when faced with a need to expand English language learning to support businesses needing to hire more people, shaping resources may involve engaging with school districts, community volunteers, and business professionals to attract and train instructors. Further efforts may involve outreach to community foundations and businesses to acquire space for one-on-one tutoring and practice, as well as obtaining laptops for use by learners. Responding together as one community to address persistent and new challenges calls for systemic collaboration.

Structuring Supports

By supports we mean policies, procedures, memoranda of understanding, and other items that clarify roles, responsibilities, and requirements in the collaborative. Developing clear and flexible working agreements including specified responsibilities, rules, and procedures can help the system adapt to emergent needs in the operating environment. Anticipating resistance to collaboration by potential collaborators with busy schedules can begin by your acknowledging up front that you understand the demanding workloads people face. You can assert that the effort of structuring supports for collaboration across systems will require work at first, but in the long run can reduce workloads for participating partners.

An example of structuring supports can be found in the area of workforce development and summer youth programs designed to introduce students to the world of work. Given the complexity of involving numerous businesses, community organizations, and schools, establishing policies, procedures, and memoranda of understanding is a necessary investment in successful collaboration. Agreements that detail who is responsible for space, training, coordination, and assigning students are essential. Further, setting forth rules and roles to ensure smooth implementation supports systemic collaboration.

Clarifying Roles

Organizational participation in a collaborative endeavor must be supported by clearly established roles that help sustain the collaboration over the long term. Ideally, roles associated with project expertise and historical background can take the form of working groups that include multiple organizational representatives. Similarly, roles pertinent to motivation and performance can be structured through working groups that expand membership and energize shared efforts through listening to clients and stakeholders. Ultimately, organizational role performance sustains systemic collaboration toward a continually evolving system that serves people and communities for the long term.

Recognizing that some collaborative ventures amount to just a few, select participants who resist involving others, it is important to design collaboratives based on a broad group of departments that commit to full engagement in the shared endeavor. Your role as a public manager involves the early engagement of meaningful, reciprocal support in collaboration. Collaboration needs to be organization-based and expansive over time, rather than limited to a select few individuals.

As an example, in an implementation team assigned to roll out a new initiative designed to increase client and community engagement, multiple collaborative roles are needed to ensure the success of the project. Expertise in outreach and interdepartmental communication, marketing, and social services, in addition to roles that incorporate critical thinking, design thinking, systems thinking, and motivation, are needed. Including staff with historical backgrounds in successful initiatives by the organization further contributes to valuable collaboration and project success.

Delivering Results

Given the prevalence of funding agencies' requiring collaboration among public organizations, some would-be collaborators may voice support, but neglect responsibilities required for effective collaborating. This can be seen in instances where organizations and their representatives demonstrate only nominal involvement and fail to respond to outreach or attend meetings consistently. A recent symptom of this pattern may take the form of people sitting in virtual meetings while texting or engaging in other activities. This contrasts with the needed engagement with other partners to advance the shared endeavor.

Your role as a public manager is to enlist every collaborating organization at the outset to be fully engaged in the shared work of the collaborative. Such engagement, entailing attendance at meetings and fiscal or other resource contributions, is critical to the success of the collaborative. Among the results of systemic collaboration are improved service quality, service completeness, and system capacity. Ultimately, collaboration exists to produce more impactful and sustained service than any one organization can deliver. Designing the collaborative toward sustained results is key to managing systemic collaboration.

An example of focusing collaborative energy toward delivering results within the organization requires setting clear expectations of every professional involved from the outset of the project. Establishing requirements associated with meeting attendance and specific contribution is imperative to successful project completion. As a public manager, you are likely to have experienced a range of commitment to collaboration in projects.

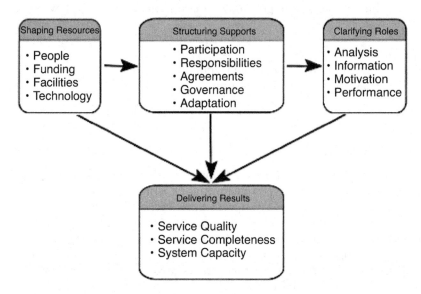

Figure 4.1 Managing Systemic Collaboration.

Setting expectations and gaining early and sustained commitment to the project also includes a role for a primary coordinator who communicates with each collaborator to support and stimulate full engagement in systemic collaboration.

A vibrant organizational system differs from a traditional organization by means of its agility, creativity, and dedication to shared purposes. Systemic collaboration facilitates the organizational system's ability to fulfill its purpose creatively, innovatively, and sustainably. Such collaboration is characterized by energy, full usage of resources, and an imaginative demonstration of commitment to the purpose within and across systems. You as a public manager encourage and build collaboration within and across organizations, often resulting in the expansion of resources (Azamela et al., 2022). Figure 4.1 depicts the key tasks of managing systemic collaboration.

Developing Relationships

Public managers at every level play a critical role in developing relationships and are responsible for clarifying the purpose(s) of the organization.

Three dimensions are important to developing relationships within a social system:

- Managing Messages.
- Building and Leveraging Social Capital.
- Inspiring Creativity and Innovation.

These three dimensions are discussed in more detail below.

Managing Messages

Regular and frequent communication regarding service delivery and opportunities to improve is fundamental to systemic collaboration. The knowledge, experience, and perspective that each collaborator brings contribute to shared understanding. Shaping messages as well as enlisting new ideas is central to developing productive relationships that focus on service quality and opportunities. Enlisting and including contributions from a wide variety of partners builds the system's capacity for evolving toward a realistic response to needs.

One way to support managing messages is to combine regularly scheduled, formal messaging such as a weekly news bulletin or directive via email, with ongoing, informal messaging. Planning informal conversations with different groups supports connection and collaboration. Maintaining two-way communication and acting upon what is learned from staff and stakeholders energizes the relationships that are fundamental to the organizational system.

Building and Leveraging Social Capital

You as a public manager are charged with building and leveraging social capital for the system. Social capital refers to accumulated value derived from trusting and cooperative relationships. These relationships support and sustain democratic values and norms as well as community solidarity and can lead to shared economic benefit over time (Putnam et al., 1994). Building social capital is the result of formal and informal relationships that facilitate connections (Hawkins & Maurer, 2012) that potentially provide practical benefits to the organizational system (Lin, 1999). Three types of social capital include (Szreter & Woolcock, 2004):

- Bonding social capital: Connecting with people who identify with similar positions, social, or economic background.
- Bridging social capital: Connecting with people who identify as having different positions, social, or economic backgrounds.
- Linking social capital: Connecting with people who differ in levels of power or authority.

Bonding and linking social capital are relevant to collaborating within systems. Bridging social capital supports collaborating across systems. Through the building of social capital, you as a public manager generate interest in and participation toward the fulfillment of shared purposes.

An example of developing bonding social capital within the organization occurs when assigning individuals with complementary skills to work together on short-term projects. One of the best ways to help people bond effectively is to provide them with practical opportunities to engage in purposeful activities to create shared results. In a similar vein, a practical way to build both bridging and linking social capital is to encourage staff to participate in external community activities such as committees where they actively work collaboratively toward a desired result with people having different backgrounds and levels of authority. These engagements shape social capital that expands the system's capacity to make productive change.

Inspiring Creativity and Innovation

An important facet of your role as public manager and communicator is inspiring creativity and innovation with internal and external professionals. Generating new ideas begins with enlisting internal staff to discover and share creative ideas for designing increasingly responsive services. Developing relationships with other professionals, community members, and business leaders who may have insights and expertise to share expands the organizational system in a valuable way (Dingler & Enkel, 2016; Szreter & Woolcock, 2004). Overall, alliances lead to strengthening the system to discover and implement new ways to ensure responsive service to people who depend on services the organizational system provides. The inspiration of creativity and innovation is central to ensuring maximum value that alliances bring to collaboration. Developing relationships in these ways and managing systemic collaboration lead to making a difference in the quality of social systems for all involved. Figure 4.2 depicts the important dimensions to developing relationships within a social system.

One approach to inspiring creativity and innovation in an internal project initiative is to propose the removal of constraints for a task force or committee working on a problem. Ask, "What if budgeting were not a problem?" to generate new ideas. Posing the question, "What if we were to deliver this service virtually and require no travel time?" can enlist new ways of thinking. Alternatively, periodically reaching out with a phone call or visit to individuals both within and outside the organization and posing a specific question, such as "Given your expertise and experience, what might you recommend we do to build interest in this new program?" can stimulate creativity in approach.

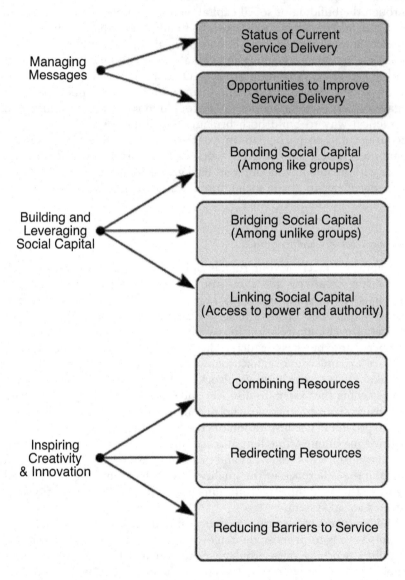

Figure 4.2 Developing Relationships for Systemic Collaboration.

Box 4.1   Theory Box: Collaborating Within and Across Systems.

A systemic thinking approach to collaboration assumes flexibility when developing and expanding resources, structures, and roles that lead to effective service. The practice of collaborating within and across systems relies on a desire to expand services and develop relationships with people and organizations. Relevant systems thinking principles, critical thinking aspects, and design thinking aspects are addressed below.

Systems Thinking Principles

Systems thinking principles were derived from original sources whenever possible. We used original sources to incorporate the history of systems thinking and to acknowledge the progenitors of the principles. The following systems thinking principles support the practice of collaborating within and across systems:

- *Communication.* The systems principle of communication pertains to sharing data, information, knowledge, and wisdom associated with the system (Checkland, 1999), such as context, processes, resources, and outcomes. This principle is especially relevant to collaboration when public managers provide frequent, clear, and inclusive communication that builds system understanding of capacity and service opportunities.
- *Emergence.* The systems principle of emergence describes a pattern of newly discovered value that arises from the collaborative integration of people, partners, resources, and communication (Checkland, 1999). Emergence represents the lively, exciting surprise factor that collaboration makes possible. In stark contrast to overly planned or micromanaged services, emergence represents the discovery of previously unknown designs and approaches to the shared purpose of the system.
- *Equifinality.* The systems principle of equifinality states that there are many ways to fulfill the system's purpose: A desired system state or goal may be achieved through multiple strategies, efforts, or means (von Bertalanffy, 1950). Resource requirements may differ, but each approach can achieve the desired result. Equifinality represents an encouraging feature of organizational systems, namely that multiple paths to achievement exist.

- *Purposeful Behavior*. The systems principle of purposeful behavior uses the system's purpose as the primary criterion for determining approaches, plans, and activity (Rosenblueth et al., 1943). Such focused behavior supports and sustains collaborative design, solution building, and service delivery. Purposeful behavior guides multiple partners to join forces to build the most effective system possible.

Critical Thinking Aspects

Critical thinking enriches collaboration by incorporating multiple stakeholders toward inclusive analysis. Over time, the collaborative entity acquires a more complete picture of challenges to address and ways to build solutions. Applying critical thinking through collaboration involves the following aspects:

- Engaging in deductive and inductive reasoning.
- Structuring arguments and supporting them with evidence.

Design Thinking Aspects

Design thinking is supported by collaboration and benefits from the inclusion of a range of perspectives as a base for exploring creative possibilities. Design thinking is composed of two cognitive processes: divergent thinking and convergent thinking. Divergent thinking is used for developing new ideas and is associated with plasticity in thinking, while convergent thinking is used to facilitate finding a clear, consensus-based solution (Zhang et al., 2020). The synthesis of divergent and convergent thinking represents the foundation of design thinking. Applying design thinking through collaboration includes the following aspects:

- Generating new ideas through brainstorming.
- Collaborating to transition from ideas to practical solutions.
- Engaging in abductive reasoning.

Case Study: A Nonprofit Executive Director Addresses Homelessness

Two versions of a case study on homelessness are presented. The first approach is non-systemic and reflects a linear way of considering the challenge. The second approach is systemic and reflects a contrasting approach to addressing the issue. While a non-systemic approach emphasizes action, this often faster, linear method may separate people from one another and miss the opportunity to convene different stakeholders of the system and effect lasting change. Systemic approaches make use of learning that derives from listening to the people we seek to serve and allows for the integration of resources in a creative manner.

Non-systemic Approach

The executive director of a nonprofit organization in a large metropolitan area with a mission to address homelessness had long recognized that the issue was having an impact on the quality of life in the community. Despite decades of service, becoming the face of the issue, and keeping abreast of current research, the director knew that the situation was clearly worsening due to economic and health issues pressuring the local area. Residents expressed fear and concern about their property values. Business owners saw that a large homeless population threatened their livelihood by discouraging people from entering their stores and offices. Elected officials in the city admitted their fear of being voted out. Police were directed to remove people from areas where unhoused individuals gathered regularly. School leaders and teachers knew that children without homes were treated poorly and wanted to support those children in their pursuit of learning in a safe place.

The executive director recognized that supportive services including mental health, childcare, and training programs were needed by unhoused people but had long known that turning things around would require a long-term effort. As a known commodity in the community, the executive director was perceived as a voice for the voiceless and an ardent promoter of their interests. She realized that her organization required more money and other resources to handle the issue effectively. Now more than ever, the nonprofit faced pressures that threatened its survival.

The executive director reached out to convene key city and county government staff, community and business leaders, other nonprofit organizations, the local community college and university representatives, and faith-based leaders to address the challenge together. A session was held to bring various perspectives to the table. The executive director began the meeting by saying, "As we all are aware, homelessness has become an even greater crisis in our community, and we need to come together and figure out what to do about it. At this time, funding has become scarce, and we all have reasons to come together and turn the situation around."

At this point, meeting attendees took it upon themselves to restate the issue in terms of what each of them faced as threats. It became clear that participants were essentially competing to express points of view that would demonstrate who was the most victimized. People stressed the horror of the situation, noting that "It has never been this bad." Speakers voiced the view that too little was being done. What used to be a challenge had only worsened to the level of a crisis.

The executive director asked people to help build a solution. At that point, each speaker recommended what she or he believed to be the simplest fix. Business owners and residents spoke about the housing shortage and stated that more low-income housing had to be authorized and built. Workforce development representatives encouraged the importance of faster ways of training and educating people experiencing homelessness, to help them gain employment. City and county staff agreed that promoting workforce development training and education to prepare people for jobs would require a longer-term solution that was worth pursuing. Retorts from multiple meeting attendees indicated impatience with all suggestions, saying, "We don't have time to wait around. This is serious. We must do something now!"

Police indicated that they could focus on areas where people without homes congregated and threaten to arrest them unless they departed the premises. A business owner offered to pay for bus tickets and provide small cash sums to people who were homeless to transport them elsewhere. Residents issued pleas to remove these individuals from their communities, based on fear for the safety of the community.

The executive director recognized that her organization was on the line regarding this situation. Residents and business owners were losing patience and claimed that the nonprofit and other organizations simply weren't doing enough. The immediate temptation was to demonstrate just how much each person was "really doing," rather than working together to create lasting solutions. The executive director recognized that no one truly knew what to do except express frustration and explore new funding to move past the pressure cooker that this issue represented.

Systemic Approach

The executive director of a nonprofit organization in a large metropolitan area with a mission to address homelessness recognized the troubling reality that the issue of homelessness had reached an inflection point in the community. The reality of the situation was that it was having an impact on the quality of life on a broad scale. She shared with staff and colleagues in the community that a focused, collaborative approach to making change was needed more than ever. She took the initiative by inviting different organizations and experts to a meeting to plan and establish a long-range community endeavor including community members and business leaders.

The goal of the meeting was to orchestrate a stronger and more unified understanding of the issue of homelessness along with other related issues that needed to be turned around. The executive director recognized that this would not involve a "quick fix," but that people needed to voice how they saw the challenge, specify what resources they believed needed to be brought together, and design a structure including complementary roles for stakeholders to support a better quality of life.

The executive director further emphasized that there likely were many appropriate ways to approach this challenge, and that no single solution would be sufficient. Further, she indicated that gaining perspectives from multiple partners working closely together would eventually provide a clearer sense of not-yet-discovered solutions based on shared ingenuity. Such system power was needed for this complex and difficult challenge.

Participants, including elected officials and business, education, and community leaders, recognized the benefit of bringing many viewpoints into the discussion and advocated an inclusive approach. The executive director planned the meeting carefully, ensuring that productive questions would guide the meeting. She set up an agenda that involved asking each attendee to describe the issue and how his or her organization could contribute to a long-term solution in combination with work from others. The executive director additionally requested that each attendee indicate what resources each organization might need to boost the effectiveness of what could become a long-term solution that would improve the quality of life for the whole community.

Unlike previous sessions, this meeting positioned people to see the challenge as a shared one with many possible ways of improving perception and contribution. For example, the local community college agreed to work with service providers to enlist unhoused people to come and enjoy a community meal and learn about support that would be made available. Other attendees spoke about supporting existing homeless shelters and building new ones. Creative ideas concerning work projects that would help people feel productive and gain access to employment were seen as ways to boost morale and shape a better future.

The executive director emphasized the importance of solutions made by all people together and of tracking small steps indicating progress as new approaches were put in place. All agreed that a positive, respectful approach to unhoused people would shift the tone away from defensive fear and negativity. Most importantly, emphasis was placed on ways for people to build and sustain support while transitioning away from feeling alone and unable to elevate themselves.

Representatives of educational institutions, healthcare organizations, law enforcement departments, faith-based organizations, and other nonprofits spoke about gaining assistance from state and local government to orchestrate medical support, nutritional meals, and assistance with schools to guide their children. Efforts were coordinated to focus on what it feels like to be in the situation of experiencing homelessness. The sharing of perspectives created a confident community mindset toward meeting the challenge.

Attendees created a support diagram that displayed the resources available to be contributed from healthcare, education, local restaurants and foodbanks, law enforcement, and multiple nonprofits. The attendees recognized what coordinated, collaborative results, tracking progress, seeking resources, and generally shaping through collaboration could accomplish over time. They agreed that intelligent pathways to improvement would help the community as a social system meet the stresses of the outer environment.

Tools

Three tools included in this chapter were designed to support collaboration:

1. The Social Capital Mapping Tool helps you as a public manager design a practical approach to building social capital.
2. The Project Roles Tool provides a vehicle that helps you design roles to structure a collaborative project.
3. The Meeting Management Checklist clarifies activities to engage in before, during, and after a meeting, to ensure effectiveness.

These tools support initial and ongoing efforts to develop collaborative relationships with staff and other stakeholders within your organization and across multiple organizations.

Social Capital Mapping Tool

The Social Capital Mapping Tool helps you as a public manager develop social capital according to the "What," "Why," "How," and "Where & When" of investment in social capital for the good of the system. Building relationships that support fulfillment of the system's purpose is at the core of collaboration. Three types of social capital are included in the Tool: Bonding, bridging, and linking social capital.

Each of the four sections at the corners of the tool provides guiding questions to help plan what you seek to achieve by building social capital, why you seek to build it, how you plan to go about expanding social capital, and specific where and when approaches. The tool provides space for naming people and organizations that represent the various aspects of social capital. See Figure 4.3.

SOCIAL CAPITAL MAPPING TOOL

Social Capital describes ways in which people relate within organizations. **Bonding** social capital is formed between members of the same organization. **Bridging** social capital is formed across organizations. **Linking** social capital is formed between those with more power or authority than those with less.

Instructions: Answer each of the questions in the corners of the tool: What, Why, How, and Where & When. Then in the Bridging and Linking sections, list the names of organizations and individuals with whom you think it would be beneficial to develop social capital.

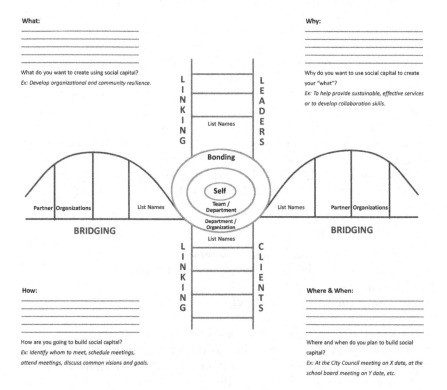

What:

What do you want to create using social capital?
Ex: Develop organizational and community resilience.

Why:

Why do you want to use social capital to create your "what"?
Ex: To help provide sustainable, effective services or to develop collaboration skills.

BRIDGING

BRIDGING

How:

How are you going to build social capital?
Ex: Identify whom to meet, schedule meetings, attend meetings, discuss common visions and goals.

Where & When:

Where and when do you plan to build social capital?
Ex: At the City Council meeting on X date, at the school board meeting on Y date, etc.

Figure 4.3 Social Capital Mapping Tool.

Source: Adapted from Szreter & Woolcock (2004)

Other Potential Uses of the Social Capital Mapping Tool

- As an assessment of the current level of social capital for you as a public manager.
- As a vehicle to help expand your engagement with clients.
- As a form for displaying a theory of change.
- As a form for capturing institutional knowledge about partners and stakeholders.
- As a strategic planning tool.

Project Roles Tool

The Project Roles Tool is used to identify and design the roles needed in a specific collaborative project. This tool allows for customizing roles to fit a particular project. Four project needs (i.e., analysis, information, motivation, and performance) call for multiple relevant roles. Analysis informs roles that entail asking questions and clarifying perspectives during dialogue about the project. Information-based roles are associated with contributing expertise and historical knowledge to the shared project. Motivation-related roles energize both internal and external dimensions for the project team. Performance-focused roles are associated with specific active contributions and innovative approaches.

Each role is described, and space is provided to identify one or more persons who will fulfill roles for the project. Project roles specify functions useful for a collaborative endeavor. Complementary roles add value to shaping the direction of a project, infusing current and historical knowledge and perspective. Roles exist to inform and enhance the results of a collaborative effort. Each role is meant to provide a facet of perspective needed to advance the project. See Figure 4.4.

Other Potential Uses of the Project Roles Tool

- As a tool for teaching project management.
- As a tool for teaching the value of individual roles, strengths, and their contributions.
- As a tool for engaging project team members to take on multiple roles.
- As a tool for learning more about staff and stakeholders.
- As a tool for facilitating group discussions based on role(s) held.
- As an external tool for managing multi-organizational collaboratives.
- As an internal tool for helping staff recognize your organization's structures, how to improve those structures and roles, and how staff and the organization could benefit by collaborating.
- As a tool for creating new roles.

Meeting Management Checklist Tool

The Meeting Management Checklist Tool is meant to be used by the person who leads a collaborative meeting. The checklist provides a simple, logical progression of steps for you as a public manager to cover before, during, and after a meeting. It is meant to guide purposeful activity that optimizes communication and fosters sustained effort toward realizing the system purpose.

PROJECT ROLES TOOL

Team projects benefit from the design of collaborative roles that support the achievement of results. Identifying roles based on project needs (i.e., Analysis, Information, Motivation, and Performance) and specifying who should perform each role contributes to the successful implementation of projects.

Instructions: Based on the project needs and roles described below, identify position title(s) or specific person(s) that should handle the responsibilities of the role described. Example: The Expert role might be assigned to the assistant director of a department. Multiple roles may be fulfilled by a single person.

Project Need			
Analysis	**Information**	**Motivation**	**Performance**
The Questioner. Provides critical thinking to ensure inclusion of multiple sides of an issue. Balances forward motion with caution and ensures comparative analysis before moving into action.	**The Expert.** Provides depth of knowledge that supports accuracy and completeness of information.	**The Appreciator.** Provides internal motivation to the team. Conveys gratitude toward project team members. Supports relationships and builds trust on the team, recognizing collaborative value and contribution.	**The Performer.** Provides direct work to the project, applying knowledge and experience to the performance of tasks that produce results.
Role filled by:	Role filled by:	Role filled by:	Role filled by:
The Clarifier. Crystallizes diverse perspectives into a message to ensure uniform understanding.	**The Historian.** Provides accumulated knowledge and practice of the organization that supports integration of current opportunities and the current record.	**The Champion.** Emphasizes external motivation in support of the team project. Applies persuasive energy and stimulates celebration of achievements to gain support for current and future projects.	**The Innovator.** Identifies, advocates, and implements new or different ways of performing tasks that support the project.
Role filled by:	Role filled by:	Role filled by:	Role filled by:

ROLE	
The Evaluator. Assesses the effectiveness of what is being done, including formative and summative results.	
Role filled by:	

Figure 4.4 Project Roles Tool.

MEETING MANAGEMENT CHECKLIST TOOL

BEFORE THE MEETING

- [ ] Design the meeting's purpose with others (always related to the System Purpose).
- [ ] Develop a clear, simple agenda using action words ("Organize," "Plan," "Review").
- [ ] Stimulate attendance through outreach to specific individuals.
- [ ] Specify and post the meeting's purpose at the top of each meeting invitation.
- [ ] Remind individuals if they have an active role in the upcoming meeting (i.e., facilitating a discussion, reporting results).

DURING THE MEETING

Beginning

- [ ] Review the System Purpose.
- [ ] Review the Meeting Agenda.
- [ ] Recap the Previous Meeting.

Middle

- [ ] Follow the agenda throughout the meeting.
- [ ] Proactively solicit input from diverse groups and individuals.
- [ ] Integrate different ideas with clarity.
- [ ] Involve meeting members in planning action.
- [ ] Collaborate on *how* to take action.
- [ ] Identify resources needed to support items under deliberation.
- [ ] Ask if there are any final comments before moving to the next agenda item.

End

- [ ] Summarize action items.
- [ ] Communicate and agree upon who will do what by when.
- [ ] Ensure that all members have specified, agreed-upon roles to perform.
- [ ] Set the time, date, purpose, and intended results of the next meeting.
- [ ] Thank participants for their collaboration during the meeting.

AFTER THE MEETING

- [ ] Document decisions and actions, specifying who will do what by when.
- [ ] Communicate with organizational leaders about meeting results.
- [ ] Coordinate meeting results with related groups in the organizational system.
- [ ] Express specific resource needs within and beyond the groups.
- [ ] Schedule activities in advance, respecting deadlines and managing deliverables.

Figure 4.5 Meeting Management Checklist Tool.

The meeting leader should share the tool with participants to ensure that all steps are addressed fully throughout the planning, the proceedings, and the follow-up period after each meeting. The tool is intended to support collaborative practice by providing a simple, easy-to-follow guide to anchor all meetings in a collaborative and effective spirit. See Figure 4.5.

Other Potential Uses of the Meeting Management Checklist Tool

- As a way of developing workforce capacity and leadership abilities in others.
- As a way of sharing facilitation duties.
- As a way of assigning duties to meeting attendees.
- As a checklist for noting what was accomplished, what worked, and what did not work during the meeting.
- As a way of managing assets during a meeting.
- As a way of ensuring that all voices in a meeting are heard.
- As a way of managing continuous improvement.

Chapter Summary

Collaboration is a practice that energizes systemic thinking by shaping resources, structuring supports, and clarifying roles to deliver effective services for those in need. You as a public manager proactively engage system partners in these activities to deliver results. Resources contributed by organizations that are part of the system include people, funding, facilities, and technology. Structured supports include participation, responsibilities, agreements, governance, and adaptation. Roles take the form of activities that support analysis, information, motivation, and performance for the collaboration. The dimensions of results include service quality, service completeness, and system capacity.

You as a public manager develop relationships that support sustained collaboration: Managing messages; building and leveraging social capital; and inspiring creativity and productivity. Managing messages emphasizes the status of current service delivery and opportunities to improve it. Building and leveraging social capital encompasses bonding, bridging, and linking social capital. Inspiring creativity and productivity entails combining resources, redirecting resources, and reducing barriers to service.

Practicing the Practice

Several suggestions are provided to help you practice collaborating within and across systems. Collaboration expands the human dimensions of public management and builds shared system understanding. Practicing collaboration builds creativity and communication as well as systemic thinking capabilities.

Exploring Approaches to Collaborating Within and Across Systems (See Case Study)

A vital aspect of your role as a public manager is to develop and build proactive collaboration that supports the evolution of the organizational system. Inclusive collaboration leads to the expansion of the system's capacity to meet new challenges in the environment. Your inviting staff and stakeholders to explore the case studies with systems thinking, critical thinking, and design thinking contributes to transforming the organizational system through the inclusion of the views of collaborative partners.

1. Review the Non-systemic Approach in the Case Study section with the meeting group and pose the following questions:

    a. How might staff, clients, and other stakeholders have reacted to the executive director's approach to addressing homelessness?
    b. What are the benefits and drawbacks to the non-systemic approach?
    c. What would you do differently to build collaborative commitment to bring about needed change in the community?

2. Request that meeting participants read the Systemic Approach in the Case Study section, and pose the following questions:

    a. How might staff, clients, and other stakeholders have reacted to the executive director's approach to addressing homelessness?
    b. What are the benefits and drawbacks to the systemic approach?
    c. What about the approach taken by the executive director would benefit our organization?

Expanding System Partnerships (See Figure 4.3)

The Social Capital Mapping Tool offers guidance for building social capital to broaden the reach and effectiveness of the organizational system. The tool helps clarify the purpose of building social capital by posing questions. You as a public manager can facilitate the intentional building of social capital by expanding awareness about its impact on the social system. Work with a group of system stakeholders to expand social capital for your system.

1. Use the Social Capital Mapping Tool to answer the "what, why, how, and where and when" questions.
2. Use the Tool to plan and build connections to support your system, including:

    a. Government agencies.
    b. Nonprofit organizations.
    c. Businesses.
    d. Educational institutions.

3. Complete the bridging section of the tool to broaden partners and supporters of the system by listing names of organizations and individuals (if known).
4. Complete the linking section of the tool to include leaders and clients to support your system by listing names of individuals.
5. Return to the "what, why, how, and where and when" questions referenced in #2 above. Discuss the appropriate next steps to develop relationships and build social capital.

Designing Project Roles (See Figure 4.4)

Use the Project Roles Tool to design the roles needed to support the achievement of results for collaborative projects. The tool specifies a range of roles that shape project success by providing expertise in needed areas. You as a public manager support the success of a collaborative project by identifying with others which roles are needed for the project in focus.

1. Identify a known challenge that can benefit from a collaborative approach.
2. Distribute the Project Roles Tool, and pose the following questions:

   a. Which of the four project needs (i.e., analysis, information, motivation, and performance) are most relevant to this challenge?
   b. Which roles in the Project Roles Tool should be filled to make this project work?
   c. What person or persons would best fill each of the needed roles? Why?

3. Assign roles so that at least one person occupies each of the roles relevant to the project.
4. Following completion of the project designed to address the challenge, ask all to share how these roles may have contributed to the project's success.

Optimizing Meetings (See Figure 4.5)

Use the Meeting Management Checklist Tool for a collaborative project meeting. Share the tool with participants prior to the meeting. Use the tool during the meeting to gain value from participants. Following the meeting, ask for feedback from participants about the meeting. Pose the following questions:

1. How effective was the meeting for achieving our purposes?
2. To what extent did we gain value from participants?
3. Who needs to be advised of the meeting's results?
4. What should be done to optimize the upcoming meeting?

Reflecting on Practicing the Practice

Reflection on the practice of collaborating within and across systems increases comprehension and can support vision and purpose fulfillment. Thinking about, writing about, and discussing the chapter, using the tools, and practicing the practice allows you to consider ways to inform and sustain collaborative strength and further develop relationships. Reflecting can take place as an individual or group activity. Consider the following questions and write or discuss your responses:

1. What worked about the practice of collaborating within and across systems?
2. What did not work about the practice?
3. What did you notice about your own thinking during the practice?
4. What did you notice about the interactions and behaviors of others?
5. What changes in collaborating within and across systems occurred as a result of practicing this practice?
6. What might you do differently the next time you practice this practice?

Recommended Readings

On Working in Groups

Coyle, D. (2018). *The culture code: The secrets of highly successful groups.* Bantam Books.

This book provides an engaging and insightful read that describes ways in which private organizations have developed teams and cultures that bring value through collaboration. Fundamental to developing effective cultures is the ability to work with others effectively in groups. The author identifies skills and practices that characterize effective work groups. We chose this book for the power and relevance of its stories that speak to collaborative cultures.

On Negotiation

Fisher, R., Ury, W., & Patton, B. (1991). *Getting to yes: Negotiating agreement without giving in* (2nd ed.). Penguin Books.

The advocated approach in this book emphasizes preserving and enhancing relationships and building mutual motivation to reach agreement rather than using harsh, combative, win-lose negotiation methods. We chose this book to support the idea that listening can be transformative and lead to creative solutions achieved with others.

On Collaborative Dialogue

Follett, M. P. (2013). *Creative experience*. Martino Publishing (Original work published 1924).

This classic in the social sciences has influenced industry leaders since the early 20th century. Follett's work clarified that a mutual understanding of each person's experience can be established through respectful dialogue: Diverse desires can be crafted into agreed-upon solutions that satisfy all parties to a greater extent than any individual solution would, while building social progress. We chose this book because of its emphasis on using the concept of difference creatively to discover with others new ideas, approaches, and pathways.

References

Aiken, M., & Hage, J. (1968). Organizational interdependence and intra-organizational structure. *American Sociological Review, 33*(6), 912–930. https://doi.org/10.2307/2092683

Azamela, J. C., Tang, Z., Owusu, A., Egala, S. B., & Bruce, E. (2022). The impact of institutional creativity and innovation capability on innovation performance of public sector organizations in Ghana. *Sustainability, 14*(3), Article 1378. https://doi.org/10.3390/su14031378

Checkland, P. (1999). *Systems thinking, systems practice: Includes a 30-year retrospective*. John Wiley & Sons.

Clarke, A., & Crane, A. (2018). Cross-sector partnerships for systemic change: Systematized literature review and agenda for further research. *Journal of Business Ethics, 150*(2), 303–313. https://doi.org/10.1007/s10551-018-3922-2

Dingler, A., & Enkel, E. (2016). Socialization and innovation: Insights from collaboration across industry boundaries. *Technological Forecasting & Social Change, 109*, 50–60. https://doi.org/10.1016/j.techfore.2016.05.017

Flanigan, S. T. (2023). Impacts of systems thinking on mission when environmental nonprofit organizations encounter the complex systems problem of homelessness. *Voluntas, 2023*. https://doi.org/10.1007/s11266-023-00577-9

Hawkins, R. L., & Maurer, K. (2012). Unravelling social capital: Disentangling a concept for social work. *The British Journal of Social Work, 42*(2), 353–370. https://doi.org/10.1093/bjsw/bcr056

Lin, N. (1999). Building a network theory of social capital. *Connections, 22*(1), 28–51. www.insna.org/connections##

Putnam, R., Leonardi, R., & Nanetti, R. Y. (1994). *Making democracy work: Civic traditions in modern Italy*. Princeton University Press.

Rosenblueth, A., Wiener, N., & Bigelow, J. (1943). Behavior, purpose and teleology. *Philosophy of Science, 10*(1), 18–24. www.jstor.org/stable/184878

San Martín Rodríguez, L., Beaulieu, M.-D., D'Amour, D., & Ferrada-Videla, M. (2005). The determinants of successful collaboration: A review of theoretical and empirical studies. *Journal of Interprofessional Care, 19*(Suppl. 1), 132–147. https://doi.org/10.1080/13561820500082677

Sandfort, J. (1999). The structural impediments to human service collaboration: Examining welfare reform at the front lines. *Social Service Review, 73*(3), 314–339. https://doi.org/10.1086/514426

Sowa, J. E. (2009). The collaboration decision in nonprofit organizations: Views from the front line. *Nonprofit and Voluntary Sector Quarterly, 38*(6), 1003–1025. https://doi.org/10.1177/0899764008325247

Szreter, S., & Woolcock, M. (2004). Health by association? Social capital, social theory, and the political economy of public health. *International Journal of Epidemiology, 33*(4), 650–667. https://doi.org/10.1093/ije/dyh013

Von Bertalanffy, L. (1950). An outline of general system theory. *The British Journal for the Philosophy of Science, 1*(2), 134–165. https://doi.org/10.1093/bjps/I.2.134

Waddock, S. A. (1991). A typology of social partnership organizations. *Administration & Society, 22*(4), 480–515. https://doi.org/10.1177/009539979102200405

Zhang, W., Sjoerds, Z., & Hommel, B. (2020). Metacontrol of human creativity: The neurocognitive mechanisms of convergent and divergent thinking. *NeuroImage, 210*, Article 116572. https://doi.org/10.1016/j.neuroimage.2020.116572

Chapter 5

Developing a Systemic Culture

A systemic culture means a culture in which people and departments are working together toward a common purpose, continuing to learn and develop themselves and their organization to serve clients more effectively. Social systems inherently involve learning and teaching to create a vibrant organization in which discovery is perpetuated throughout the systemic culture. A key to this learning and teaching is discovery, where people engage in conversations, activities, and ideas through natural inquisitiveness and curiosity.

In contrast, bureaucratic organizations are less interested in engaging in discovery, learning, and teaching. Bureaucratic organizations, at their worst, are more interested in uncovering compliance issues and correcting employees' mistakes, causing them to learn to fear making errors. That is not what we mean by discovery, teaching, or learning. While compliance certainly has its place in a social system, it is not the purpose of the organization. Rather, compliance is part of the organization's structure and serves as one of the organization's functions.

Developing an organizational culture generally involves two schools of thought: Structural and cultural. There are those who see culture as emanating from organizational structures, such as hierarchies. An example of a structural approach to developing a culture would be to focus on improving structures within the organization (e.g., policies, procedures, and processes), causing the culture to shift as a result of those improvements. One assumption behind the structuralist approach is that the thinking that occurred when the structure was built was, and still is, sufficient for culture development.

There are also those who see culture development as a more direct activity (i.e., changing the culture itself). A cultural approach to developing a culture may mean focusing on employee motivation or leadership development, for example. An assumption behind the culturalist approach is that to change something, you need to focus on it.

Moynihan and Landuyt (2009) explored discordant views between structuralists and culturalists about the source of workplace learning. As

DOI: 10.4324/9781003335153-5

described in their study, structuralists believe that learning arises from an organization's structures, such as training processes or communication channels. Culturalists, in turn, believe that learning arises from the organization's culture, such as one of open-mindedness or employee empowerment.

After surveying employees from 53 state agencies within Texas, Moynihan and Landuyt (2009) found that variables affecting workplace learning include *both* structural and cultural elements. We argue that culture development is a form of learning, and that learning includes both structural and cultural elements. But how do you as a public manager go about developing a systemic culture, and how much does learning have to do with it?

About the Practice

Structure

Developing a systemic culture begins by understanding the current organizational structure. This is more complex than simply labeling the organizational structure as a hierarchy or networked organization because most public organizations use multiple forms of structures to govern or manage. For example, a city government might be organized as a hierarchy with the city manager at the top of the organizational pyramid, but it likely also utilizes public-private partnerships, another structural form.

Mintzberg (1996) argued that democratic government organizations are often structured as bureaucratic hierarchies or as business-like performance organizations, neither of which serve social system clients well. He asserted that public-private partnerships are a step in the right direction, but ultimately may wind up being a mere combination of the bureaucracies and private companies. Networked organizations that collaborate freely represent progress, he thought, but one step further would be what we refer to as social systems. Figure 5.1 depicts the types of organizational structures based on Mintzberg's (1996) ideas.

Figure 5.1 displays the types of organizational structures along two axes. The x-axis ranges from a focus on compliance to a focus on clients, and the y-axis ranges from an environment of control to one of creativity. Nearing the meeting point of a focus on clients and an environment of creativity lies the structure of social systems.

Mintzberg (1996) discussed five primary elements of social systems, described here as Engagement, Interaction, Instruction, Dependability, and Acuity:

- Engagement refers to recruiting and retaining employees based on their values and dispositions, at least as much as their skill sets and education.
- Interaction means actively paying attention to how and why people work together.

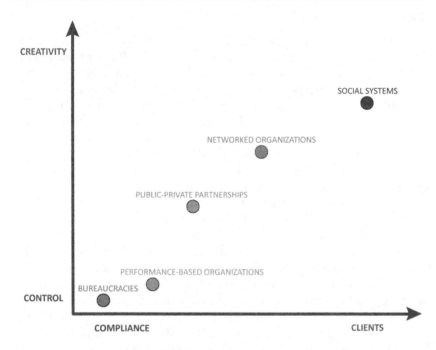

Figure 5.1 Types of Organizational Structures.
Source: Adapted from Mintzberg (1996)

- Instruction means setting performance metrics aside and instead help-ing employees make connections between their values, what is being worked on or learned (e.g., systems principles), and the organization's purpose.
- Dependability is an explicit value of being trustworthy and reliable that is practiced by all and expected by all and encourages authentic development.
- Finally, acuity refers to the respected input provided by those with experience and a stake in the outcome (i.e., managers, select peers of employees, and clients).

As noted earlier, public organizations use most types of organizational structures (bureaucracies, performance-based organizations, public-pri-vate partnerships, and networked organizations) in their daily activities. We agree with Mintzberg (1996) when he suggested that while operating within the larger system of a democracy, we would all be better served if the social system structure were given more attention than the bureaucratic or performance-based structures.

Culture

Why develop or change an organization's culture at all? Setting aside whether change emanates from structure or culture itself, the broader question of why change occurs in an organization is a compelling one to ponder. Research on organizational change has explored this question more in depth. Ashworth et al. (2009) suggest there are two reasons why public organizations change: (1) to produce better results or (2) to comply with outside pressure. Institutional theory suggests that organizations change in response to pressures from outside the organization, such as regulatory pressure, political pressure, or pressure from peer organizations. The theory also states that an organization will comply with those pressures out of a concern for its survival as an institution (Ashworth et al., 2009). Institutional theory thus seems to describe the reactive versus proactive nature often encountered in public management.

However, a reactive state is not always negative. With respect to the organizational structures based on Mintzberg's (1996) ideas presented in Figure 5.1, it took a great investment of time and energy to get government organizations to shift from bureaucracies to performance-management organizations. Another outcome of that investment was an increased number of public-private partnerships. Due to global challenges such as poverty, human rights abuses, and climate change, pressure is mounting on the public sector to structure more networked organizations and social systems.

Performance Culture

The era of New Public Management (NPM), implemented in the United States by the Clinton Administration in the late 1990s, had much to do with the pressure to move government from bureaucratic to performance-based structures. During the NPM movement scholars were studying the benefits of using data to manage performance in the public sector with programs like CitiStat in Baltimore (Abramson & Behn, 2006; Behn, 2007). The effectiveness and growth of this and other work helped to establish performance-based organizations as one of the predominant structures in the public sector.

Performance-based work (Behn, 2003; Abramson & Behn, 2006; Behn, 2007) helped inspire related research such as that of Moynihan et al. (2020), who surveyed public managers in healthcare to discover how they use performance data. Moynihan and colleagues were interested in how public managers' use of performance data would impact the goal-based learning of public professionals in healthcare, such as physicians and nurses. The primary findings indicated that when public managers used performance data to solve problems, there was an increase in goal-based learning by healthcare professionals. And when public managers used data to reward or control employees, that learning decreased. The authors acknowledged other uses of performance data, such as educating an organization's leadership and stakeholders, and noted that most public managers are aware of the multiple ways in which they use performance data and information (Moynihan et al., 2020). Managing performance is an important part of developing a systemic culture, and we believe that it can be a strength when used within a social system. The balance required when moving between social systems' structures and other structures while developing a systemic culture can be achieved and maintained by identifying and managing how public managers use performance data and information. We will revisit these ideas in the Tools section of this chapter.

Systemic Culture

A systemic culture is one in which systems thinking, critical thinking, and design thinking are used and encouraged. Systemic thinking requires us to consider the environment (e.g., social, political, economic, ecological) in which the organization is situated, to learn how the environment affects the organization and vice versa, and to consider ways in which that relationship could more effectively serve clients and the general public. Institutional theory limits the external pressures to political or other-organizational, and therefore does not account for the myriad of challenges experienced today.

In their classic work, DiMaggio and Powell (1983) discussed how an organization's environment pressures it to conform to political or legislative will, or to converge with other organizations (i.e., conduct benchmarking), or to become like other professionals in their associations, thus producing a paradox: The more organizations try to change, the more alike they become. Schön (1971) described an example of this phenomenon when he discussed organizations that submitted grant applications in which the authors promised to comply with federal regulations in order to receive the funds, then returned to business as usual, doing what they wanted to do, ignoring the pressure to conform. In their study of local English governments, Ashworth et al. (2009) described organizations as being compliant with outside regulations while internally expressing defiance.

Defiance does not have to be underhanded or covert. Overcoming conformity can often be accomplished through the ongoing practice of diversity, equity, inclusion, and accessibility (DEIA). Systemic thinking supports DEIA efforts by allowing people and organizations to express themselves and their ideas without succumbing to unnecessary pressures to conform. Systems thinking calls for the collection of diverse perspectives and the inclusion of them when addressing systemic concerns. Critical thinking acts as a pivot point and regulates systems thinking so it doesn't go too far by resulting in more conformity (such as in a bureaucratic or performance-based environment). Design thinking then picks up the ideas discovered by systems thinking and critical thinking and synthesizes the pieces into new ideas and forms that may take shape as policies, programs, products, or processes. Through design thinking, we understand that compliance and innovation are not mutually exclusive.

A systemic approach to culture development also allows for the inclusion of democratic values. Kernaghan (2000) discussed the potency of values in public organizations and suggested that public managers need to beware of democratic values being taken over by private sector values—particularly in performance-based organizations. Some examples of democratic values include integrity, equality, justice, civic duty and pride, freedom (e.g., speech, religion, press), diversity, unity, neutrality, and the balance of power. Kernaghan (2000) then discussed the importance of managing public values as a priority over rule-following behavior and suggested that cultures may be transformed through values rather than structures. The controversies and conflicts surrounding democratic values are also included in social systems. Finding ways to express democratic values, to listen for their expression, and to resolve the inevitable conflicts that arise due to their expression is part of the process of developing a systemic culture in public organizations.

Developing a Systemic Culture

Developing a systemic culture is a continual, iterative process that involves several steps:

- *Discovering.* The purpose of discovery is to identify what the current culture is and how it does or does not connect with the larger system purpose. Discovery often involves qualitative study and data collection, such as one-on-one interviews with employees, peers, leaders, and clients.
- *Analyzing.* Analysis involves a review of the data collected from multiple sources during the discovery step. One way to analyze is first to sort the data according to similarities you see, then use critical thinking to identify any assumptions that may underlie what interviewees said to you. Finally, allow yourself to see patterns emerge.
- *Synthesizing.* Synthesis involves reviewing the similarities and emergent patterns and then allowing yourself to use design thinking to recognize and form these into broader themes. These resultant themes should capture the spirit of the culture you and others currently experience.
- *Connecting.* Connecting involves taking a succinct statement about the current culture and building a verbal bridge between it and the systemic culture being developed. This may occur by first using design thinking to connect your analysis with your system's purpose. Then create concise ways of communicating your synthesized connections.
- *Educating.* Educating involves communicating the connections you designed to as many people and in as many ways as possible within your organization. Be prepared to answer questions about your discovery

and analysis steps and be open to including any feedback you receive into subsequent synthesizing.

- *Modeling.* Modeling in this context is a form of educating that involves behavior and affect. People watch what managers do and how they seem to be—more than they listen to what managers say. It is important to have an authentic and ongoing interest in developing a systemic culture so as to "walk the talk."

Managers at every level of the organization have a role in developing a systemic culture that cannot be overstated. Proactive communication and leading learning in the organization are of paramount importance. For example, professional development is a form of learning that occurs in organizations, and public managers can have a hand in shaping it as a tool for culture development. Realizing that adult learning requires patience, compassion, and an appreciation of employees' experience and expertise (Knowles, 1972; MacKeracher, 2004), you as a public manager can strive to ensure that professional development opportunities are truly valuable and support systemic culture building. Your role as a public manager also includes the responsibility to appreciate the value of DEIA throughout the system; to see diversity, equity, inclusion, and accessibility as gifts to a vibrant organization. A diagram of developing a systemic culture is depicted in Figure 5.2.

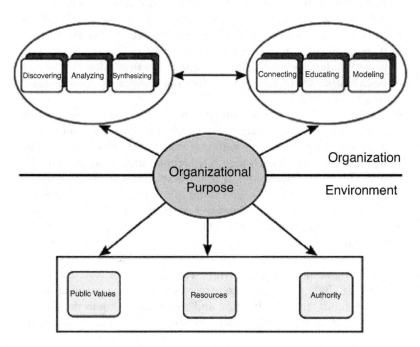

Figure 5.2 Developing a Systemic Culture.

Box 5.1   Theory Box: Developing a Systemic Culture.

A systemic thinking approach to the development of the organization's culture supports consideration of the impact of multiple factors at once: The environment, learning (through structural and cultural elements), leadership, and values. The practice of developing a systemic culture relies on learning and communicating. Relevant systems thinking principles, critical thinking aspects, and design thinking aspects of systemic thinking are described below.

Systems Thinking Principles

Systems thinking principles were derived from original sources whenever possible. We used original sources to incorporate the history of systems thinking and to acknowledge the progenitors of the principles. The following systems thinking principles support the practice of developing a systemic culture:

- *Feedback.* Feedback is communication about actions, behavior, or performance that is intended to guide future actions, behavior, or performance (Wiener, 1954). Regular meetings with individuals to obtain and deliver feedback are highly recommended, as they provide ideal opportunities to learn about individuals' thinking, skills, values, and goals. In subsequent meetings, discussions can be held about how a person's values might relate to the organization's purpose(s).
- *Relaxation Time.* Relaxation time is the time needed to recover from a change or disorder that disturbs the system's equilibrium, after which characteristic behavior resumes (Loehle, 2018). This means that when developing a systemic culture, we need to be mindful of the psychological drain that comes from constant or multiple change efforts. We should allow for times when people do not have to concern themselves with change.
- *Basins of Stability.* It is important to be aware that people will gravitate toward what attracts them (i.e., what they are familiar with). Building upon research conducted by Menck et al. (2013) and Leng et al. (2016), an awareness of basins of stability means that big changes require extensive resources (e.g., training, time, effort, funds) to shift attention and create attraction to the desired change or new plateau (basin). In other words, if change efforts

are not provided with sufficient resources and attention, people may return to prior habits and behaviors.

Critical Thinking Aspects

Critical thinking supports the development of a systemic culture through the use of language and the development of discernment. Critical thinking further benefits the development of a systemic culture by using various formats and purposes of communication and by discerning the values expressed in messages. Critical thinking aspects were derived from works based on the reasoning and logic of the Ancient Greeks as well as on those concerned with the design of public social systems. The following key aspects of critical thinking support the development of a systemic culture:

- *Developing Rhetorical Expertise.* Rhetoric is the skilled application of linguistic expression (Herrick, 2021). Written and audial/visual forms of language may be used for purposes of advocacy, persuasion, argumentation, compliance, etc. Rhetoric is a form of communication that may be designed with good or bad intentions, based on democratic or other values. It is important to study the rhetoric you and others use, understand why it's being used, and recognize the effects that may result.
- *Analysis* is the process of breaking down larger components into smaller parts (Gharajedaghi, 2011; Nelson & Stolterman, 2014) for the purposes of study and better understanding. Analysis is useful in numerous ways: When discerning fact from opinion, making decisions, identifying groupthink, etc. Groupthink describes the negative result arising from having greater concern for conforming with and justifying group decisions than with allowing new, alternative, or contrary ideas to be considered (Diestler, 2020; Janis, 1982). Analysis helps you as a public manager maintain your awareness of the dangers of groupthink, supports your analysis of what drives your and others' decisions, and may prompt the courage to question decisions, authority, or the status quo.

Design Thinking Aspects

Design thinking aspects support the development of a systemic culture by focusing on the recipients of the message. Design thinking also supports systemic culture development by emphasizing the positive aspects of communication and ensuring their inclusion. Design thinking aspects were derived from the works of authors concerned with their application in the public sector in general and social systems in particular. The following key aspects of design thinking support the development of a systemic culture:

- *Listening* is where design thinking begins (Nelson & Stolterman, 2014) and is arguably the most important element of it. In the context of developing a systemic culture, listening is key to helping staff make connections between their work, democratic values, and system purposes. Simply listening for these connections when meeting with staff, other managers, or leadership during the course of a day will reveal opportunities for further development.
- *Synthesizing* is a primary activity in designing and refers to the act of bringing seemingly disparate elements together (Buchanan, 1992; Gharajedaghi, 2011; Nelson & Stolterman, 2014). For example, synthesizing may occur as a result of reflection following conversations with multiple employees and reading various documents. In the context of developing a systemic culture, synthesis may be used to create a simple and inclusive message about culture development to be delivered in team, department, and organization meetings.

Case Study: A State Child Welfare Manager Addresses the Need for Change

A case study focused on organizational culture development is presented to illustrate two ways of approaching the issue. The first is a non-systemic, linear-analytical approach and reflects a deductively constructed way of perceiving the challenge. While deductive thinking is valid and valuable, the second, systemic approach also reflects an inductively and abductively constructed way of perceiving the issue.

Non-systemic Approach

A new manager recently appointed to lead a state agency responsible for serving young abuse victims faced considerable challenges. The manager understood that the agency had recently received considerable negative press based on its failure to handle and respond to thousands of cases of abused children. The manager recognized that his appointment to the top management post in the agency resulted from the need by the governor to demonstrate immediate attention to a crisis. The governor's firing of the previous manager was intended to convey that oversight of the agency had been ineffective and unacceptable.

Feeling the pressure of the situation, and recognizing that time was of the essence, the new manager assembled his direct reports and asked them to "drill down" in each of their respective areas and analyze how cases were being managed. The goal was to identify points of failure in addition to purported patterns of success by individuals seen to be performing their jobs well. The primary focus was on identifying gaps and filling them. Any identified individual failure was seen as grounds for termination. Identifying scapegoats would buy time and presumably instill public confidence that something was being done. Likewise, looking for "most valuable players" was seen as the flip side of this linear approach.

Thinking deductively was comfortable for the new manager. Getting to the bottom of who was making mistakes and "letting heads roll" as well as finding out who was performing effectively was a pattern he knew well, based on his many years with the agency. In fact, that experience brought him close to the realization that no one was or should be safe from public scrutiny. He gave his direct reports plenty of leeway to ferret out trouble and to find who was at fault.

The new manager placed himself at the center of the challenge, communicating in direct terms that he was in charge and personally stood for finding out mistakes and eradicating corruption. Staff in the organization showed signs of being fearful for their jobs and committed to demonstrating that they had been following policy and procedures as they had been taught. The defense of one's actions often also meant covering one's tracks. Most staff members not only were defensive but also felt separated from their colleagues, holding out the hope of saving themselves amid what was likely to be an escalating environment of casting blame.

As each reporting supervisor discovered mistakes, successive firings took place, each of which added fuel to the fear-based scenario. Few professionals felt comfortable taking proactive approaches to serving their clients. Staff feared that stepping out in any way would likely result in the loss of their jobs. Virtually no one was willing to risk their career in face of the pressure felt throughout the organization. Despite the identification of good performers, the attention given to these individuals paled in comparison to the harsh firings. As might be predicted, some of the first professionals who decided to leave the agency on their own were those perceived by staff as the best qualified and top performers in the agency. Management was not concerned about this adverse effect and continued to press on, indulging themselves in what they perceived as their power to make fast and needed change.

The net result of the analytical approach revealed a weakness in the organization's culture. Once the furor of the rapid-fire, mistake-finding mission was concluded, what had the new manager created? In fact, he had dismantled the organization and lost a considerable store of institutional knowledge and capacity. The presumed merits of cleaning house and starting over were based on an assumption that became an illusion. Whatever experiential knowledge base had been present before had now been taken down and disparaged. In addition, the unintended or ill-considered consequence of chasing away the best performers who preferred not to work in a negative environment was brought to reality. The emphasis on breaking down the organization according to individual performance and looking at people separately from the organization inevitably resulted in a loss of value for the organization as a system.

Systemic Approach

A new manager was appointed at the time of a public relations crisis for a social service agency at the state level. Recent negative press resulted in her appointment as the lead officer of the agency. Although she had been part of the agency for many years, her new position would offer her a different perspective, and she determined to learn as much as she could about the strengths and capacities that she and members of the organizational system had to work with. She recognized that the unfortunate circumstances that resulted in her appointment required clarity and action by all members of the organizational system.

The manager used her own knowledge of the organization to prepare several questions. She sought input from her direct reports on the questions she had drafted and refined those questions prior to scheduling appointments with her direct reports and their staff as well. She personally captured notes during each interview, explaining to interviewees that she wanted to learn from their answers and from others' answers. She told them that once she had interviewed all parties, she would consolidate what she heard into a document that she would share with the entire organization.

Following her interview with each direct report, the manager shared that she wanted to interview everyone in the organization. She was adamant in her belief that the caliber of systemic thinking in the organization depended on diversity, equity, inclusion, and accessibility. It was her contention that to ensure accuracy of perspective, the greatest range of diverse views was necessary. The manager commented to her close associates that some individuals charged with leading and guiding an organization make the mistake of tolerating staff opinions rather than welcoming them. The manager perceived that seeking agreement amounted to robbing the organization of its greatest richness: The diverse range of viewpoints needed to make a great and sustained organization. Meeting clients' needs made this imperative.

The approach taken by the manager when scheduling these meetings differed from previous patterns that had occurred in the organization. Instead of calling interviewees to her office, she scheduled the meetings in their private offices or conference rooms close to where each person worked. She wanted to send a message of respect as she engaged in listening to each person's views.

Upon completion of the interviews, the manager crafted a document to share with everyone in the organization during one large meeting. She consolidated the viewpoints she heard regarding how staff members perceived the organization's purpose. She further shared an integrated view of how the parts of the organization worked together and connected. She included input regarding not only staff members of the organization but partnering organizations who surely were part of the system.

Included in the exploration were questions concerning how performance was measured and should be measured, to ensure strong focus on the clients being served by the organizational system. The manager discovered from her interviewing process a great richness of talent, some of it not applied sufficiently to support the organization's purposes. Further, she noted among staff a universally strong desire to help clients. The importance of connecting parts of the organization and its partners together revealed many opportunities to strengthen ties. Included in these opportunities was the need for more lateral communication and relevant projects that would encompass creative ways of combining resources of the organization's departments and those of partner organizations. Further, client perspectives needed to be better integrated into the organization's understanding. Interview findings also revealed the need to educate the legislature regarding how this state agency compared to those in other states, with an emphasis on opportunities for improved service to clients.

The manager conducted an all-employee meeting and began by presenting a synthesis of perspectives that staff provided during interviews. The manager presented a welcome finding: Interviews revealed a sense of connectivity and commitment by staff. Two areas of opportunity emerged: Strengthening the organization's capacity for learning and specifying the most appropriate metrics for the agency. Staff were asked to participate in follow-up meetings of small groups to discuss and settle on the details of these opportunities.

The manager emphasized that the organization had a great deal of talent with which to build a strong and connected culture around its shared purpose. She encouraged staff to connect with partners and to structure ways to include partners as vital parts of the organizational system that existed to serve clients. She indicated that the job would require effort from all working together, never competing against one another for attention, but always in the spirit of service to the many clients.

Of key importance was placing the issue heightened by the press in proper context. Rather than treating the emergency as the sole focus, the manager sought to establish, with others, ways to preclude the concerning pattern and recognize how specific linkages among departments would furnish critical information well ahead of creating a crisis. She recognized that strengthening the behavior and functionality of the organization as a system was more valuable and productive than engaging in fear-based activities that would reduce the capability of the organization to do its best work. She also realized that developing a systemic culture takes time and that the cycle of development would be continuous and evolutionary.

Tools

The three tools included in this chapter were designed to support the development of a systemic culture through direct and indirect requests for feedback:

1. The Social System Survey.
2. The Social System Scorecard.
3. The Systemic Knowledge Wheel.

The first two tools, the Social System Survey and the Social System Scorecard, work together to provide a snapshot of the culture as it currently is. The third tool, the Systemic Knowledge Wheel, is intended to facilitate a transition from a performance-based culture to a systemic culture.

The Social System Survey Tool

Communicating information about your organization as a social system is one of the simplest and most effective ways to build a systemic culture. The Social System Survey is a ten-question survey asking employees their opinions about how effectively information about the system is communicated and to what degree employees and clients engage with that information. Allow employees to remain anonymous when completing the survey, and let employees know the survey will be conducted once or twice each year. The survey is depicted in Figure 5.3.

The survey may be distributed in paper and pencil format, or it may be distributed using online survey software of the reader's choice. Calculations involve averaging the score for each of the ten questions. In general, the higher the score, the more positively your organization functions as a social system.

SOCIAL SYSTEM SURVEY TOOL

Please indicate your level of agreement or disagreement with the following statements:

1. Our organization's mission and vision are easy to convey to others.

(1) Disagree strongly   (2) Disagree Somewhat   (3) Neutral   (4) Agree Somewhat   (5) Agree Strongly

2. This organization communicates the good it does to members of the community though data and stories.

(1) Disagree strongly   (2) Disagree Somewhat   (3) Neutral   (4) Agree Somewhat   (5) Agree Strongly

3. People in the community trust our organization.

(1) Disagree strongly   (2) Disagree Somewhat   (3) Neutral   (4) Agree Somewhat   (5) Agree Strongly

4. At our organization we continuously find ways to simplify processes for our clients.

(1) Disagree strongly   (2) Disagree Somewhat   (3) Neutral   (4) Agree Somewhat   (5) Agree Strongly

5. Management communicates the full cycle of projects (beginning, middle, and end results).

(1) Disagree strongly   (2) Disagree Somewhat   (3) Neutral   (4) Agree Somewhat   (5) Agree Strongly

6. Management uses different communication strategies with different groups of people either inside or outside this organization.

(1) Disagree strongly   (2) Disagree Somewhat   (3) Neutral   (4) Agree Somewhat   (5) Agree Strongly

7. Visuals are often used to communicate messages about the organization.

(1) Disagree strongly   (2) Disagree Somewhat   (3) Neutral   (4) Agree Somewhat   (5) Agree Strongly

8. Data are used to communicate important and relevant information in my department.

(1) Disagree strongly   (2) Disagree Somewhat   (3) Neutral   (4) Agree Somewhat   (5) Agree Strongly

9. I am provided opportunities to participate in organizational problem-solving activities or projects.

(1) Disagree strongly   (2) Disagree Somewhat   (3) Neutral   (4) Agree Somewhat   (5) Agree Strongly

10. I am able to manage and organize the information I receive at work.

(1) Disagree strongly   (2) Disagree Somewhat   (3) Neutral   (4) Agree Somewhat   (5) Agree Strongly

Figure 5.3 Social System Survey Tool.

Other Potential Uses of the Social System Survey Tool

- As a way to gauge progress of program evaluation or other projects.
- As a form to solicit feedback from clients or stakeholders.
- As the first step in an improvement process.

The Social System Scorecard Tool

The second tool, the Social System Scorecard, is used to track results from the Social System Survey over time. The scorecard allows for quick and simple recognition of where gaps may exist and points to areas of opportunity for further development.

This tool was designed to track results of the two most recent administrations of the survey using the "Current Score" and "Previous Score" columns. Current Score—Previous Score = the score that gets recorded in the "Change" column. For example, a + 0.5 in the Change column would indicate a half-point increase over the previous score. Just as with the Social System Survey Tool, the higher the score, the more positively your organization is moving toward becoming a social system.

The "Survey Item" column on the scorecard tool is a reminder of which question was being asked. The scorecard also contains a column entitled "Cultural Construct" that notes the type of communication each item measures. Finally, the column entitled "Operational Construct" indicates which organizational process each item supports. The scorecard is depicted in Figure 5.4.

The Systemic Knowledge Wheel Tool

The Systemic Knowledge Wheel Tool was developed to help public managers shift their workplace from a performance-based organizational structure to a social system structure. The tool was designed to provide public managers with an understanding of how they use performance information. Performance information is what managers glean from performance data through an analysis of the data. As discussed earlier in this chapter, public managers use performance information in several ways, such as solving problems or controlling performance by rewarding and penalizing employees. The Systemic Knowledge Wheel Tool is depicted in Figure 5.5, and an example is provided in Figure 5.6. Instructions for using the tool are described below.

1. *Set the time frame for measurement.* When using this tool, first determine the time frame during which you will track the number of times you use performance information. Insert the dates of your time frame near the top of the tool's page. For example:

    a. If you want to do an initial test of the tool, you may want to set the time frame as one week.

SOCIAL SYSTEM SCORECARD TOOL

Group that completed the Social System Survey (staff, managers, etc.): _____

Purpose: To record results from the Social System Survey Tool.

Instructions: Record the cumulative average score for each survey item in the boxes below and note the date administered. Note whether there was an increase or decrease in each survey item's score. Reflect on the implications of the cultural and operational constructs of each score.

SURVEY ITEM	PREVIOUS SCORE ___/___/___	CURRENT SCORE ___/___/___	CHANGE + / –	CULTURAL CONSTRUCT	OPERATIONAL CONSTRUCT
1. The mission and vision are easy to convey to others.				Clear Communication	Retention
2. The organization communicates the good it does using data and stories.				Building Trust through Communication	Recruitment
3. People in the community trust the organization.				Building Trust through Communication	Recruitment
4. The organization simplifies processes for clients.				Building Trust through Communication	Retention
5. Management communicates the full cycle of a project.				Complete Communication	Roles
6. Management uses different strategies to communicate with different groups of people.				Strategic Communication	Roles
7. Visuals are used to communicate information.				Clear Communication	Development
8. Data are used to communicate information.				Accurate Communication	Development
9. Respondents have opportunities to participate in problem-solving activities.				Participatory Communication	Development
10. Respondents are able to manage and organize information.				Efficient Communication	Development

Figure 5.4 Social System Scorecard Tool.

    b. If you are ready to do a more thorough examination, set the time frame as one month.

    c. To gain a more complete picture, one quarter may be the appropriate time frame.

2. *Track the frequency of occasions.* Next, fill in the appropriate sections after each occasion on which you use performance information. What

SYSTEMIC KNOWLEDGE WHEEL TOOL

From date   To date

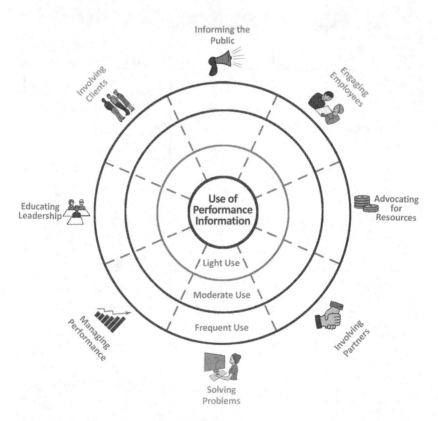

Figure 5.5 Systemic Knowledge Wheel Tool.

Source: Adapted from Moynihan et al. (2020)

you're measuring is the number of times you use performance information. (Each of the examples below corresponds with the filled-in Systemic Knowledge Wheel in Figure 5.6.)

a. For example, if you refer to performance information while speaking
with employees in individual meetings to discuss their performance
and you held four of such meetings, you will go to the "Managing

SYSTEMIC KNOWLEDGE WHEEL TOOL

July / 1 /25   Sept. /30/ 25

From date   **To date**

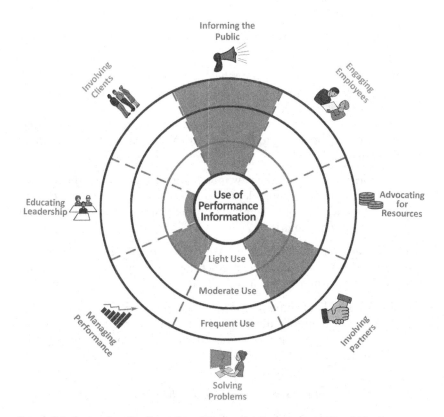

Figure 5.6 Example of a Completed Systemic Knowledge Wheel Tool.
Source: Adapted from Moynihan et al. (2020)

Performance" pie piece and shade in the area closest to the center circle, indicating light use.

b. Another example would be after several meetings held with partners and one with the state legislature in which you discussed performance information. You would go the sections, "Involving Partners" and "Educating Leadership" and fill in those sections accordingly, indicating moderate use with partners and light use with the legislature.

c. A further example pertains to the wheel section, "Informing the Public." After a series of town hall meetings, focus groups, etc., you would fill in that section accordingly, indicating frequent use.

d. It is important to note that "Moderate Use" is not necessarily better than light use, and "Frequent Use" is not necessarily better than moderate use. What is important is to track how you use performance information.

3. *Consider the whole.* After tracking the frequency of use, consider the whole wheel.

a. Were there any parts of the wheel left out? Was that because there were no interactions, was it because performance data was not necessary, or were there other reasons?

b. What could be done to engage those missing parts of the wheel? What could be done to incorporate performance information in those areas?

4. *Repeat the process.* With the new information gleaned from the tool, set a new timeframe, put your ideas into action, and track the next cycle. We recommend keeping this tracking process simple and easy so that it becomes nearly automatic.

5. *Developing systemic knowledge.* After a few tracking cycles, consider exploring ways in which more interactions might take place. For example, look at the outer edges of the wheel:

a. How might clients interact more with leadership?

b. How might the public inform you as the public manager?

c. How might these types of information build knowledge about the system?

Other Potential Uses of the Systemic Knowledge Wheel Tool

• As a project management communication tool.
• As a management tool for multiple projects.
• As a reminder of the many parts of a project and system.
• As a teaching tool for systemic management.

Chapter Summary

Developing a systemic culture begins with an awareness of the structural and cultural aspects of the organization. Understanding and teaching systems thinking principles and aspects of critical thinking and design thinking supports this awareness. When developing a systemic culture, the role of the manager at any level of the organization is to be responsible for human learning and development. With human learning and development as a foundation, public managers are able to take the culture-building steps of discovery, analysis, synthesis, connection, education, and modeling to complete the first of many cycles of development.

A systemic culture is a dynamic reality that strengthens a response to the shared challenge of delivering services to clients. A purpose-driven culture depends on the active contributions of all stakeholders in the organizational system, whose diverse views provide important insights that build the upward trajectory of a vibrant organization. In a dynamic environment, the organization is continually transforming in innovative ways.

Practicing the Practice

Several suggestions are provided to help you expand the practice of developing a systemic culture. Developing a systemic culture is at the core of creating a vibrant organization. Engaging staff and stakeholders in sharing insights, generating new ideas, and shaping a connected and purposeful culture becomes a way of life that facilitates the continual evolution of the system.

Exploring Approaches to Developing a Systemic Culture (See Case Study)

You as a public manager set the tone for the culture of the organizational system. Building on the strengths and knowledge of staff and stakeholders as vital assets of the system represents an investment in the system. The practice of developing a systemic culture positions the organization to meet challenges comprehensively. Inviting staff to apply their systems thinking, critical thinking, and design thinking to the case studies helps staff explore ways of approaching challenging situations from a position of strength.

1. Review the Non-systemic Approach in the Case Study section during a meeting and pose these questions:

    a. How would staff, clients, and other stakeholders react to the culture that the state manager created when faced with a significant challenge in the environment?
    b. What are some of the benefits and drawbacks of the culture described by the state agency?
    c. What might you do differently to shape a culture capable of responding to the challenge described?

2. Request that meeting participants read the Systemic Approach in the Case Study section, and pose the following questions:

   a. How might the staff, clients, and other stakeholders react to the culture described?

   b. What are some of the benefits and drawbacks to the culture described in the state agency?

   c. What about the approach used by the state manager would benefit our own organization?

Supporting Systemic Culture Development (See Figures 5.3 and 5.4)

The Social System Survey Tool and the Social System Scorecard Tool measure several critical dimensions that support culture development in a social system. The tools provide public managers with an indication of employee perceptions about critical indicators at a point in time. Findings provide a basis for transforming the organization to become more systemic and connected around shared purposes. The tools further facilitate communication with staff and stakeholders about opportunities for change. Using the Social System Survey and Scorecard Tools:

1. Establish a date for administering the survey to obtain baseline data on critical indicators.
2. Communicate with employees the importance of the survey for measuring how the organizational system communicates information to support culture development.
3. Send the survey to employees with a requested date for completion.
4. Calculate the scores on the survey for each dimension (i.e., produce an average score for each question).
5. Hold a meeting with all employees to share the results of the Social System Survey using the Scorecard.

   a. Share positive measures.

   b. Share opportunities for the organization to improve.

   c. Ask employees for their ideas:

      i. On how to build upon the positives.

      ii. On how to improve in categories that indicate room for change.

   d. Document the input received.

   e. Share that the survey will be administered again in six months or a year to provide time for continued work on culture development.

6. Hold a separate meeting with team leaders, supervisors, and other managers to design a plan for integrating employee ideas that support systemic culture development.

Developing Systemic Knowledge: Time Allocation (See Figures 5.5 and 5.6)

The Systemic Knowledge Wheel Tool offers a way for public managers to see and track how time is allocated to each of the eight focal areas included in the tool. How public managers allocate their time to develop a systemic culture is important. The tool facilitates new approaches to time allocation and shaping activities that support a systemic culture.

1. Consider the current time commitment you make to each of the eight focal areas included in the Tool.
2. For each category, fill in relevant sections of the wheel according to the following:

   a. Light Use = Minimal time commitment
   b. Moderate Use = Moderate time commitment
   c. Frequent Use = Extensive time commitment.

3. Notice where you currently invest the greatest amount of your time.
4. Ask yourself the following questions:

   a. Is the current time allocation to the various categories effective for supporting a systemic culture?
   b. What, if anything, would be a better allocation of your time? How would you distribute your time among the categories of supporting a systemic culture?

Reflecting on Practicing the Practice

Reflection on the practice of developing a systemic culture enriches understanding and awareness. Thinking about, writing about, and discussing the chapter, using the tools, and practicing the practice allows you to consider ways to make sustainable positive change in your culture. Reflecting can take place as an individual or group activity. Consider the following questions and write or discuss your responses:

1. What worked about the practice of developing a systemic culture?
2. What did not work about the practice?
3. What did you notice about your own thinking during the practice?
4. What did you notice about the interactions and behaviors of others?

5. What developments in the culture occurred as a result of practicing this practice?
6. What might you do differently the next time you practice this practice?

Recommended Readings

On Leadership

Kouzes, J. M., & Posner, B. Z. (2007). *The leadership challenge* (4th ed.). John Wiley & Sons.

Kouzes and Posner researched behaviors that effective leaders have in common, and they describe each in this book. This work has several editions. We chose the 4th edition because it contains a useful exercise on determining one's personal values.

On Learning

Dweck, C. S. (2016). *Mindset: The new psychology of success* (Updated ed.). Ballantine Books.

This book describes Dweck's well-known research into how people perceive learning and intellect and how we can become more aware of and resolve our limiting perceptions. We chose this book because of its simplicity and power to transform the individual reader.

National Academies of Sciences, Engineering, and Medicine. (2018). *How people learn II: Learners, contexts, and cultures*. National Academies Press. https://doi.org/10.17226/24783

This book provides a comprehensive review of the literature on teaching and learning throughout life. We chose this book because of its information on experts versus novices, adult learning, and the influence of culture on learning.

On Education

Freire, P. (2015). *Pedagogy of the oppressed*. Bloomsbury Academic (Original work published 1970).

This book discusses the power of learning, advocacy, and the dignity of equality. This is a classic work that unapologetically stands with the poor and marginalized. We chose this book because of its ability to explore and expose assumptions within systems and provide ways of thinking to transform them.

References

Abramson, M. A., & Behn, R. D. (2006). The varieties of CitiStat. *Public Administration Review, 66*(3), 332–340. https://doi.org/10.1111/j.1540-6210.2006.00592.x
Ashworth, R., Boyne, G., & Delbridge, R. (2009). Escape from the iron cage? Organizational change and isomorphic pressures in the public sector. *Journal*

of *Public Administration Research and Theory*, 19(1), 165–187. https://doi. org/10.1093/jopart/mum038

Behn, R. D. (2003). Why measure performance? Different purposes require different measures. *Public Administration Review*, 63(5), 586–606. https://doi. org/10.1111/1540-6210.00322

Behn, R. D. (2007). *What all mayors would like to know about Baltimore's CitiStat performance strategy.* IBM Center for the Business of Government. https://web. pdx.edu/~stipakb/download/PerfMeasures/CitiStatPerformanceStrategy.pdf

Buchanan, R. (1992). Wicked problems in design thinking. *Design Issues*, 8(2), 5–21. https://doi.org/10.2307/1511637

Diestler, S. (2020). *Becoming a critical thinker: A user-friendly manual* (7th ed.). Pearson Education.

DiMaggio, P. J., & Powell, W. W. (1983). The iron cage revisited: Institutional isomorphism and collective rationality in organizational fields. *American Sociological Review*, 48(2), 147–160. https://doi.org/10.2307/2095101

Gharajedaghi, J. (2011). *Systems thinking: Managing chaos and complexity: A platform for designing business architecture* (3rd ed.). Morgan Kaufmann.

Herrick, J. A. (2021). *The history and theory of rhetoric: An introduction* (7th ed.). Routledge.

Janis, I. L. (1982). *Groupthink: Psychological studies of policy decisions and fiascoes* (2nd ed.). Houghton Mifflin Company.

Kernaghan, K. (2000). The post-bureaucratic organization and public sector values. *International Review of Administrative Sciences*, 66(1), 91–104. https://doi. org/10.1177/0020852300661008

Knowles, M. S. (1972). Innovations in teaching styles and approaches based upon adult learning. *Journal of Education for Social Work*, 8(2), 32–39. https://doi. org/10.1080/00220612.1972.10671913

Leng, S., Lin, W., & Kurths, J. (2016). Basin stability in delayed dynamics. *Scientific Reports*, 6, Article 21449. https://doi.org/10.1038/srep21449

Loehle, C. (2018). Disequilibrium and relaxation times for species responses to climate change. *Ecological Modelling*, 384, 23–29. https://doi.org/10.1016/j. ecolmodel.2018.06.004

MacKeracher, D. (2004). *Making sense of adult learning* (2nd ed.). University of Toronto Press.

Menck, P. J., Heitzig, J., Marwan, N., & Kurths, J. (2013). How basin stability complements the linear-stability paradigm. *Nature Physics*, 9(2), 89–92. https:// doi.org/10.1038/nphys2516

Mintzberg, H. (1996). Managing government: Governing management. *Harvard Business Review*, 74(3), 75–83.

Moynihan, D. P., Baekgaard, M., & Jakobsen, M. L. (2020). Tackling the performance regime paradox: A problem-solving approach engages professional goal-based learning. *Public Administration Review*, 80(6), 1001–1010. https://doi. org/10.1111/puar.13142

Moynihan, D. P., & Landuyt, N. (2009). How do public organizations learn? Bridging cultural and structural perspectives. *Public Administration Review*, 69(6), 1097–1105. https://doi.org/10.1111/j.1540-6210.2009.02067.x

Nelson, H. G., & Stolterman, E. (2014). *The design way: Intentional change in an unpredictable world*. The MIT Press.

Schön, D. A. (1971). *Beyond the stable state*. W. W. Norton & Company.

Wiener, N. (1954). *The human use of human beings: Cybernetics and society*. Da Capo Press. (Original work published 1950).

Chapter 6

Designing a Systemic Future

Designing a systemic future means focusing on what can be created in the present that will support inclusive, ongoing, and sustainable service to clients and communities. Designing a systemic future means that you as a public manager are prepared to handle complexity, such as wicked or ill-structured problems, and previously unforeseen events as they occur. It also means that you are developing your ability to anticipate the occurrence of complex eventualities and using your design skills to create proactively what communities truly need and want. Finally, designing a systemic future means that your work as a public manager in the present intentionally builds the future while considering the past.

In contrast to a design thinking approach to a systemic future, a more common practice in public organizations has been to engage in a strategic planning process. Strategic planning typically focuses first on the past, then moves to the future, and then is implemented in the present. Often, strategic planning is a solely analytical approach to future-building that typically lacks a theoretical foundation (Borins, 2010; Brown, 2010). The final stages of strategic planning usually include presentations to stakeholders, followed by an implementation process that may be weak (Carvalho et al., 2022), resulting in little to no change occurring. Strategic planning is still an important facet of organizational life, however, requiring valuable skills such as strategic thinking, trend analysis, and quantitative data analysis.

Design thinking in the public sector has become more commonplace since Simon (1996) introduced the idea in the 1960s. Schön (1971) suggested that complexity and uncertainty were becoming standard challenges for public managers, in part due to the incongruity between government institutions and the societal problems they are meant to solve. Rittel and Webber (1973) asserted that design thinking would be useful when handling the complex or wicked problems of the public sector.

Design thinking and research have since evolved to include trial-and-error experimentation such as pilot testing (Bason, 2014) and prototypes (McGann et al., 2018). More recent design thinking approaches

DOI: 10.4324/9781003335153-6

have noted the importance of the use of empathy in the design process (Bason, 2014; Boland & Collopy, 2004; Nelson & Stolterman, 2014) and the inclusion of all stakeholders (Carvalho et al., 2022; Lafontaine & Lafontaine, 2019; Nzewi et al., 2022; Scott et al., 2018, 2021; Zhu et al., 2021). Interest in the application of design thinking in the public sector has also led to the development of municipal policy labs (McGann et al., 2018; Olejniczak et al., 2020).

Overall, the progress of design thinking and systemic design thinking has been limited by their use as problem-solving or problem-structuring approaches (Nelson & Stolterman, 2014). However, a systemic design thinking approach has developed in recent years, taking the whole system into account (Nelson & Stolterman, 2014) when designing policies (Schön, 1983). Systemic design thinking in the public sector has room to evolve, perhaps due to the restrictive nature of regulations and the requirements for planning already in place. But how do you design a systemic future in the public sector when there are restrictions, regulations, and planning processes to deal with?

About the Practice

The act of designing is founded on the intentions of bringing improvements to the world, serving people (Boland & Collopy, 2004; Nelson & Stolterman, 2014), and creating more meaning in life (Nelson & Stolterman, 2014). Designing is both an applied art and an applied science (Simon, 1996). To design is to use knowledge, skills, and practices to create something new (i.e., processes, policies, programs, and systems). Designing is a practice akin to management, as both begin by dealing with matters as they are in the present (Boland & Collopy, 2004; Nelson & Stolterman, 2014). As such, the act of designing aligns well with the work of those who serve in social systems.

The types of design most often used in public organizations do not result in products one would find in a room, but less obvious things related to processes and systems such as policy designs and organizational designs. Policy designs involve the crafting of language to set the rules and regulations that govern how a system or service will operate. Organizational designs are comprised of structural designs, process designs, and procedural designs that control how day-to-day operations are managed. Service design concerns the design of offerings to clients, including program design.

Systemic design offers a way to manage complexity (Nelson, 2007). Systemic design is a way of being continuously aware of the holistic nature and needs of an organization (Nelson & Stolterman, 2014; Schön, 1983). Systemic design is a process of improvement, adaptation, or innovation that begins with listening (Nelson & Stolterman, 2014), develops ideas in connection with a system's purpose, and ends with learning from the implementation of those ideas (Boland & Collopy, 2004).

Many authors have described the process of designing, for example, in literature on design-based research methods (Easterday et al., 2018; IDEO. org, 2015; McKenney & Reeves, 2019). While useful, these works do not discuss designing a systemic future for an organization, nor do they address the inclusion of democratic values when designing public sector systems. Democratic values provide the foundation of every design in the public sector and were discussed in Chapter 5 as an important aspect of developing the systemic culture of a public organization (Kernaghan, 2000). Values such as equality, justice, service, and representativeness are relevant to the design of social systems. Designing a systemic future in public organizations means including the conceptual nature and complexity inherent in social systems while grounding designs in democratic values.

Enacting the Practice of Designing a Systemic Future

Enacting the practice of designing a systemic future consists of seven iterative stages. Research on learning tells us that experts have more contextual background to draw upon, and their approach to new situations is more flexible than that of novices (National Academies of Sciences, Engineering, and Medicine, 2000). Public managers have varying degrees of expertise; therefore, the seven stages of design are not necessarily completed in the order listed, nor must each stage receive equal time and consideration. However, it is important that each stage be completed authentically and with integrity at least once during each cycle. Each stage of the practice is described in more detail below and outlined in Figure 6.1.

Listening

Listening is the act of giving your full attention to another person in order to receive their message. Listening is where designing always begins (Nelson & Stolterman, 2014). Listening arises from a genuine curiosity about another person, their experiences, and what they have to say. Curiosity stems from open-mindedness, a sense of wonder, and a desire to learn.

Listening adds value by authentically including all stakeholders. Authentic inclusivity means that all stakeholders are heard, especially clients who are not typically included (Boland & Collopy, 2004) and stakeholders who are responsible for implementing the design (Carvalho et al., 2022; Zhu et al., 2021). If clients' wants and needs are not heard, the design will not be complete (Nelson, 2007), and if the implementers of the design are not included, the design risks not coming to fruition (Carvalho et al., 2022).

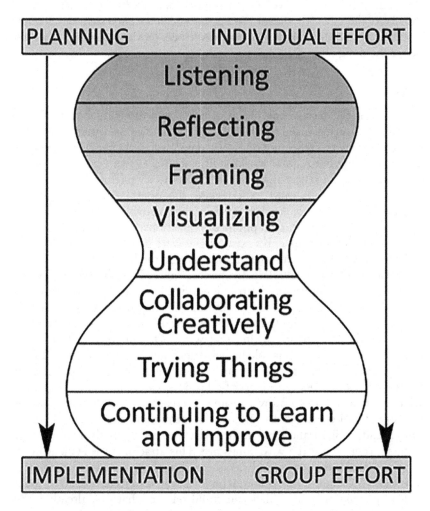

PLANNING   INDIVIDUAL EFFORT

Listening

Reflecting

Framing

Visualizing
to
Understand

Collaborating
Creatively

Trying Things

Continuing to Learn
and Improve

IMPLEMENTATION   GROUP EFFORT

Figure 6.1 Seven Stages in the Practice of Designing a Systemic Future.
Source: Adapted from Nelson & Stolterman (2014); Schön (1983)

Respect is integral to listening as it is the basis of forming lasting relationships. Changes in relationships can affect the outcomes (Boland & Collopy, 2004) of social systems. Relationships with stakeholders develop from a foundation of intentional respect: For people as fellow human beings, for stakeholder contributions and feedback, and for their work on collaborative projects.

Listening also involves empathy: The ability to place yourself in someone else's world and experience life as they experience it. Designing something meaningful for people involves the use of empathy. Listening with empathy elicits the most important data upon which social system designs and systemic futures are based. The better one becomes at being empathic, the better the design.

Reflecting

Reflecting is the active exploration of one's own thoughts with the intention of discovering insights and shaping ideas. You as a public manager engage in the act of reflecting on issues, data, programs, processes, policies, etc., as part of your regular working life (Schön, 1983).

Other areas to reflect upon when designing a systemic future include clients' wants, needs, and experiences; the organization as a system; and democratic values. As democratic values provide the foundation for designing a systemic future in public organizations, it is important to begin to learn what values currently exist, which were used to create the system, and which will best sustain the organization in the future.

It is also important to relate democratic values to one's own role within the system. The importance of role identification was discussed in Chapter 4. When designing a systemic future, reflecting on your role is vitally important. It is important to think about how others see your role and how transparently you perform it. In other words, it is important for the purpose of reflection that your role be performed authentically (Schön, 1983).

The idea of authentic role performance is related to the next reflection item: Reflecting about letting go of what is already known. Letting go of what is already known allows room for creativity and new possibilities (Nelson & Stolterman, 2014). It does not mean that a person should intentionally adopt ignorance, but rather that they let go of their attachment to being right about the way things are. This attachment is evident in the refrain, "That's the way it's always been done here." Reflecting on areas in which you might hold such attachments may lead to letting go of them.

Recognizing areas in which you could release what you already know will help you perform the next task in this stage: Reflecting on assumptions. Assumptions are notoriously difficult to identify; as they are often so pervasive, they can be likened to the air we breathe or the water we swim in. Assumptions become the basis of constructed social realities. Unfortunately, assumptions are frequently insidious in nature, resulting in systemic stasis rather than systemic futures. Identifying assumptions and reflecting upon them is a critical thinking step that facilitates shifting them toward more inclusive, sustainable realities. Later in the chapter, we provide a tool for identifying and transcending assumptions.

Reflecting about time and sustainable futures includes learning from past mistakes and taking proper action in the present. Considering ways to make services sustainable, or to make clients self-sustaining, represent examples of future-based reflection. Looking back on what has worked well in the past or learning from past mistakes is always important. Occurrences that capture employees' and others' attention in the present are also worthy of reflection.

Finally, reflecting on opportunities is the cognitive foundation on which the process of designing takes shape. Opportunity reflection helps shift the organization as a system away from past-based, rote decision-making into an enlivened future- and present-based proactive creation. Reflecting on what could be, on what is desired, rather than on problems to solve or what is merely needed (Nelson & Stolterman, 2014; Nelson, 2007) brings the design process to life.

Framing

Framing is a form of focused reflection (Schön, 1983) that involves placing a problem, situation, challenge, or project within a relatable context to prompt insights, possible courses of action, or even solutions. Frames may also be considered a form of assumption or social construction that, if not identified, promote the need to maintain the status quo, thereby limiting one's options and abilities to create (Schön, 1983; Vickers, 1983a). Alternatively, when a public manager engages in framing, they begin to see a number of options, thus developing their creative abilities (Schön, 1983).

Framing includes the tasks of analysis and synthesis discussed in Chapters 2 and 5. It includes the tasks of foregrounding, in which certain elements of a situation or project are paid more attention, and backgrounding, in which other elements receive less attention (Nelson & Stolterman, 2014; Vickers, 1983a). Framing involves reshaping, which is simply a way of fine-tuning or massaging one's thinking about a subject, and recontextualizing. Recontextualizing places the situation or issue against a new mental background that reveals how the issue might be affected.

Visualizing to Understand

Visualizing to understand refers to the act of depicting a system by eliciting and synthesizing input from multiple stakeholders. Depicting the system was discussed at length in Chapter 2. When designing a systemic future, we suggest using the system depiction you previously developed with stakeholders as a prompt for discussions about the system and ways to redesign it. Stakeholders' input will lead to the updating of your existing visualization.

In some situations, you may develop a new visualization. For example, you may want to create a new depiction that bounds the system at the service level or program level to provide more detail about what is working and not working for clients and employees. Collaborative visualization allows for efficient and effective communication about the system and provides the initial design input that sets the transformational process in motion (Boardman & Sauser, 2013; Boland & Collopy, 2004; Checkland, 1999; Nelson, 2007; Nelson & Stolterman, 2014; Schön, 1983).

Feedback obtained using the system depiction helps you as a public manager learn and understand more clearly where stakeholders are coming from. During discussions using the visuals, you may also discover assumptions that have constrained stakeholder actions or currently constrain your own organization. Feedback should be incorporated into the visual to update it. The process of sharing system depictions, obtaining feedback, updating, and re-sharing should be repeated as needed.

Collaborating Creatively

Collaborating creatively means working with like-minded and diverse thinkers to develop a new systemic design (e.g., process, service, program, policy). Collaboration was discussed extensively in Chapter 4. With respect to designing a systemic future, collaborating creatively includes several tasks, the first of which is recognizing system constraints (e.g., budget limitations or performance metrics). As Boland and Collopy (2004) pointed out, managers typically try to find workarounds for constraints rather than face them. However, constraints are inherently part of public policy issues (Simon, 1996) and can often spur creativity. The point of understanding constraints is to agree on where the boundaries for the design lie, then to discuss whether to adhere to them, push back against them, or ignore them (Boland & Collopy, 2004).

The next task in collaborating creatively involves using visualizations; either those that already exist or new ones developed for this stage. Visualizations should be used within the collaboration as artifacts to prompt discussion and ideas, thus leading to the task of discussing possibilities (Kaplan, 2011; Miettinen & Virkkunen, 2005; Werle & Seidl, 2015). Discussing possibilities can be prompted by asking What if? questions (Schön, 1983). Examples of "What if?" questions include: "What if funding were not an issue?" "What if we changed that policy?" "What if we could combine our services?"

Once possibilities have been discussed, including possible next steps, the next logical task is to communicate with leadership. Maintaining frequent communication with leadership when designing a systemic future is integral to the process. Leadership may serve as your greatest support, or leaders may need to learn more before providing their approval for projects.

Finally, when collaborating in any situation, especially when creating something new, it is important to remain positive. Creativity gets thwarted in negative environments and around negative attitudes (Staw et al., 1981; van der Voet & Lems, 2022). Staying positive is supported by looking first at what works about an idea. Some public managers might even hold entire meetings in which only the positive aspects of ideas are discussed.

Positivity also affects the ability to recognize opportunities, which is key to the final task of allowing emergence. When ideas start to flow, people often build upon what others have said before. Design is about bringing together diverse ideas, perspectives, realities, and constraints and allowing new holistic, composite ideas to emerge through synthesis (Buchanan, 1992; Gharajedaghi, 2011, Nelson & Stolterman, 2014). Collaborative creativity helps keep the system's purpose top of mind and promotes seeing the big picture as well as the smaller details.

Trying Things

Trying things means implementing something new and seeing what does or does not work. The tasks involved in this stage begin with developing prototypes and experimenting. Prototypes are usable examples of an idea that clients or other stakeholders can examine and try out for themselves. Examples of prototypes might include a new process, new policy, or new program. Experimenting may mean trying the prototype with stakeholders, or it may mean conducting a pilot study (e.g., trying a small version of a new program with new policies and processes with a limited group of people). Trying things requires accepting that there will be successes and failures: It is important to learn from both.

The next tasks in the trying things stage include implementing and evaluating. These are tasks familiar to public managers that also apply when designing a systemic future. Implementation means the prototype or pilot study is ready to be used by the stakeholders served. Evaluating designs includes assessing the feasibility and desirability (Boardman & Sauser, 2013; Checkland, 1999; Checkland & Poulter, 2020) of the program, process, policy, etc. Evaluating also involves obtaining more feedback from stakeholders. Data collected to evaluate the design ideally should include both qualitative and quantitative data to provide a more systemic perspective (Vickers, 1983b). However, take care not to let people become too focused on the numbers. The point of interviewing clients and listening with empathy is to see the system from their perspective, respect it, and act to change it for the better—for them. Start there. Return to that point frequently. This lets them know you value them and are responsive to their needs.

The final tasks in the trying-things stage are redesigning and retrying. Redesigning involves returning to the design with input collected from an evaluation and making the necessary changes. Retrying is the task of developing a new prototype or undertaking a new experiment.

Continuing to Learn and Improve

Continuing to learn and improve is the final stage in the process of designing a systemic future. The process of designing a systemic future is never finished. Of course, new designs will be implemented, and we expect circumstances to change, people to develop, and societies to evolve. We also expect to learn from these alterations and to adapt, making designing a continuous process from which to learn (Nelson & Stolterman, 2014; Schön, 1983).

The tasks included in this stage require maintaining patience with the practice of designing a systemic future. This is important because the practice is ongoing, and because of the all-too-often slow pace of public sector bureaucracies. Expect to encounter bureaucratic obstacles, necessitating patience. The final task in this phase supports continuity: Repeating the process. Repeating the process may mean completing another cycle with your current design project or it may mean repeating the process in another area of your organization as a system.

Box 6.1   Theory Box: Designing a Systemic Future.

In this section, we focus on design thinking and critical thinking, while systems thinking is placed in the background. A systemic thinking approach to designing a systemic future supports creativity, inspiration, and a desire to produce. The practice of designing a systemic future is propelled by a profound desire to listen, learn, and serve (Nelson & Stolterman, 2014; Schön, 1983). Design thinking aspects, critical thinking aspects, and systems thinking principles that are useful to the practice of designing a systemic future are described below.

Design Thinking Aspects

Design thinking aspects support the design of a systemic future by allowing control over complexity rather than becoming overwhelmed by it. Design thinking also supports the design of a systemic future by allowing access to more effective service and spurring insight into the social systems' foundations to ensure the sustainability of democratic values. Design thinking aspects were derived from works by authors interested in their application in the public sector in general and social systems in particular. The following key aspects of design thinking support the design of a systemic future:

- *Imagination.* Imagination is the act of making mental pictures. For the purpose of designing a systemic future, this ability is especially relevant to the creative aspects of designing. The ability to imagine makes contemplating sustainable futures possible. Imagination is distinct from creativity. Creativity may bring forth the ideas, but it is imagination that helps shape ideas into visual forms that can become realities (Nelson & Stolterman, 2014).
- *Innovation.* Innovation is what results once creativity and imagination have been realized and utilized in a new design (Nelson & Stolterman, 2014; Vickers, 1983a). Innovation is less conceptual and more practical than creativity or imagination. Innovation is also more skill- and experience-based; it is more systematic than systemic in nature (Vickers, 1983a) and is especially relevant to the implementation stage of designing.

Critical Thinking Aspects

Critical thinking supports the design of a systemic future by addressing the assumptions that have covertly driven the organization. Critical thinking also supports the design of a systemic future by encouraging the inspection of thoughts, opinions, suggestions, or plans. Critical thinking aspects were derived from works based on the reasoning and logic of the Ancient Greeks. The following key aspects of critical thinking support the design of a systemic future:

- *Identifying Assumptions.* Assumptions are what lie beneath arguments, actions, plans, policies, programs, services, constitutions, organizations, etc., in the public sector. The identification of assumptions paves the way for the design of sustainable social systems. Programs or policies that are built on weak, invalid, outdated, or faulty assumptions will not be effective (Diestler, 2020).
- *Testing Ideas.* Questioning is a simple form of testing ideas. The testing of ideas is an important tenet of a democratic society (Herrick, 2021), and questioning is crucial to identifying assumptions. Testing ideas, like listening, represents an overarching aspect of designing a systemic future.

Systems Thinking Principles

Systems thinking principles were derived from original sources whenever possible. We used original sources to incorporate the history of systems thinking and to acknowledge the progenitors of the principles. The following systems thinking principles support the practice of designing a systemic future:

- *Law of Consequent Production.* Building upon the critical thinking aspects noted earlier, the law of consequent production states that a system can only produce what it produces (Calida et al., 2016). Systems should be examined critically and compared with how the system is represented. Put another way, systems may become ineffective because they suffer from inauthentic execution of their designs. Restoring social systems' effectiveness may occur by clearly identifying what is being produced and then working backward to what was intended in the original system design. Taking such steps may reveal many unnecessary or inauthentic policies, practices, and processes; it may also reveal faulty assumptions.
- *Multi-tier Thinking.* This is a process that goes beyond thinking about hierarchies, or levels of staff, management, and leadership in an organization. A system is not just a collection of individual elements acting independently. In the larger framework of a system, individual parts behave differently and undergo changes when interacting at the level of the system itself: These interactions bring about new properties for the system (Wilenksy & Resnick, 1999). Multi-tier thinking may be as simple as reminding ourselves that the whole system has different properties from those of a collection of individual parts acting alone.

Case Study: A County Hospital Administrator Guides the Design of the Future

A case study focused on designing a systemic future is presented to illustrate two ways of approaching an issue. The first example applies a non-systemic, linear-analytical approach and emphasizes a business-based, primarily quantitative focus. The second example uses an inclusive approach to designing a systemic future that recognizes complexity and reflects participation, empathy, and democratic values.

Non-systemic Approach

The administrator of a county hospital recognized an opportunity to establish a new vision for the future of the hospital. An influx of new "big name" private hospitals in the local area meant less attention being paid to this long-standing hospital. It was feared that this situation might affect the hospital's ability to attract and retain highly qualified staff.

The administrator and staff believed that the county hospital should be perceived as one that served the broader community rather than exclusively lower socioeconomic patients. The specialty services for which the hospital was generally known included family medical care, emergency services, and addiction services, in addition to advanced surgical services. The administrator believed that emphasizing best practices in service would heighten public understanding of the value of the hospital's range of offerings. The administrator voiced her view that putting in place a primarily quantitative, results-oriented, and business-focused approach, emphasizing year-over-year performance metrics, would be beneficial and demonstrate tight procedures, fiscal soundness, and responsive service.

It was determined that developing a new strategic plan would be timely, offer a convenient way to show "who we are," and help the community understand what a great provider of services the hospital was. The administrator convened her direct reports and instructed them to prepare for the creation of a new strategic plan. She emphasized that showcasing the many hospital services in the plan and establishing tight and clear metrics would offer a results-based, quantitatively-focused strategic plan that would stimulate staff to deliver effective services. With board support, the administrator agreed that this was exactly what was needed and directed department heads to contract with a facilitator to guide the process.

The decision was made to conduct a two-day strategic planning session that would be held at a nearby resort where board members and senior staff could stay overnight if they wished. Senior staff hired a facilitator and advised that individual to lead the group in establishing a business-focused strategic plan. The facilitator was instructed to make the plan direct, specific, and quantitative, and ensure that no extraneous "clutter" would obfuscate the plan. With this directive, the facilitator expressed that a precise strategic plan that mimicked private sector practice would be very doable. The facilitator proceeded to develop an agenda for the two-day session.

Day one of the strategic planning session proved to be a busy one. The administrator, board members, and senior staff shaped a vision and mission, along with clear, measurable goals and supporting strategies. Following prompts by the facilitator, participants in the strategic planning session began developing metrics that would facilitate quarterly results for each of the hospital departments. It was agreed that every department manager would come before the administrator and board on a quarterly basis and defend his or her staff's performance. Board members and the administrator could question performance and "ask hard questions" of each department head. Budgetary performance would be included in the quarterly reviews. The metrics put in place would also guide staff performance evaluations.

After two days of detailed planning, the facilitator prepared a written summary of the strategic plan and distributed it to all participants. The administrator announced that each department head would convene his or her staff and share the strategic plan. She shared that each department head should emphasize to staff that their input would be welcomed. Each department head proceeded to schedule staff meetings to convey the new strategic plan and gather responses from employees.

Systemic Approach

Upon deep and extended reflection, the long-serving administrator of a county hospital recognized an opportunity to envision a new reality for the hospital. Over the past decade, she and her senior staff had developed a clear sense of the hospital's identity in the community. Senior staff were consistently active in community associations and took part in initiatives that extended beyond the hospital's walls.

Recent economic trends, including a downturn in the state and local economies, meant that services and outreach had become more community-centered and less exclusively medical in nature. The administrator, well liked and respected as a leader, understood intuitively that things had changed and that this long-standing hospital had come to be a trusted and important institution in the community. This was especially the case for vulnerable populations, who relied upon the hospital as a safe and accessible location for receiving a wide range of needed services. It had become clear to the administrator that the organizational system was characterized by complexity, and she perceived an opportunity to design a systemic future for the institution.

The administrator understood that designing a systemic future would require a different approach from previous efforts to reconfigure or re-envision the hospital. Business-styled strategic planning, a regular occurrence every three to five years, meant a repeated process that typically revealed only surface level change. As part of the administrator's active engagement with the community, she sensed that the hospital had become a complex, multi-faceted system. The roles of staff, board, and stakeholders had changed and led to a new, yet unarticulated, identity for the hospital in the community.

It now was time to bring together the many different parts of healthcare and community services that comprised a system. Despite years of linear, analytical approaches, the administrator perceived an opportunity to look at the hospital differently and more inclusively. She decided to engage in a series of individual and small group conversations with staff at all levels of the hospital, asking questions, listening intently to what professionals shared, and capturing notes about the learning that emerged. As she listened to a diverse range of views from staff, representatives of numerous nonprofit organizations, government, and university partners, as well as patients and patient families, she began to understand more clearly that the hospital comprised more than a medical facility, but a broader social system.

She asked herself: What if the hospital community looked at designing a systemic future as one vast group of people mutually connected who shared a dedication to intentional, responsive service? The administrator recognized the nature of traditional strategic planning, a primarily top-down way of perceiving an organization's work and service. In the current world, beset by health crises, a systemic approach would likely lead to a proactive, anticipatory style of services and programs that would more effectively serve the public.

The more she listened, the more she became aware that running the hospital was in fact systemic and egalitarian rather than vertical and authoritarian. Multiple experts and numerous people receiving services helped capture a broader, deeper vision. Several themes emerged from the conversations.

One theme involved the availability of hospital staff and other providers required to handle both emergency and non-emergency situations. How effectively were we attracting and retaining capable and committed staff to be part of the system? Another theme pertained to how decisions at the hospital were made and who was included in making those decisions. Third, having a visual depiction of the county hospital as a system would provide a clear and concrete picture. This picture would be useful for helping stakeholders recognize current and potential ways of connecting people, policies, and services.

As the administrator continued her meetings with stakeholders, including partner providers of services, such as addiction counseling and family mental health support; board members; hospital staff; and patients and families, she captured notes about how the system appeared based on what she heard. She sketched the system on paper, showing the purposes of the hospital, the groups providing services, and the way that these groups and services were connected. Following initial interviews, the administrator shared hand-drawn sketches with multiple people and asked them, "Is this an accurate depiction of who we are as a system?"

With each shared iteration, she heard changes and refinements from staff and stakeholders, and thereby gained greater clarity and understanding. Representatives of nonprofits providing mental health services added further detail to her initial diagrams. Physicians and nurses emphasized the importance of connecting with service professionals to complete the cycle of care with patients and families. A particularly telling finding was that the hospital needed to devote greater attention to potential health crises and prepare for them, rather than merely reacting to new challenges that emerged.

The administrator refined the draft diagram she had gathered and asked small groups of people to respond to three questions: (1) Is this an accurate picture of what we do and how we do it? (2) How could we design our system to be more responsive and innovative? (3) How would that look on our diagram? The groups often included people with different roles who shared with one another ways of making the current diagram more accurate. They also offered suggestions for making possible innovations. Finally, they reshaped the visual diagram to show different connections and relationships that supported an inclusive, transformative living system.

The administrator began to realize that serving in a systemic organization was far different from what was done in a traditional organization. It meant bringing forward the many experts and people benefiting from the system and finding new ways to serve more comprehensively. The visual depiction of the system stimulated ideas and spawned design thinking.

Designing a systemic future transcended the level of a simple strategic plan and served as an evolutionary, energizing, collaborative exploration and discovery in which people engaged in shared learning. That learning was translated over time into a new pattern of service design and delivery. The individuals and organizations involved consistently expressed excitement about being included, having their views shape the design, and indicating that they "could not wait" to try some of the new ideas presented. The visual continued to be a conversation starter that sparked ideas and stimulated deep and extensive thought among members of the system.

As stakeholders of the hospital system experimented with new programs and services, policy changes, process redesigns, and service program redesigns came to life. No one considered any effort to be "just one thing." Instead, each new approach to healthcare services led naturally to the question, "What else might we be able to do to serve our community in a systemic way?"

Tools

The three tools included in this chapter were designed to support designing a systemic future:

1. Identifying and Transcending Assumptions Tool.
2. Principles for Systemic Design Thinking Tool.
3. Implementation Ideas Checklist Tool.

These tools were developed to be used during one or more of the Seven Stages in the Practice of Designing a Systemic Future (Figure 6.1).

Identifying and Transcending Assumptions Tool

Identifying assumptions is similar to looking at the blueprints that formed the organization as a system. Identifying and transcending assumptions involves examining the values, habits, or learned limitations that resulted in the current state of the system. The identification of assumptions is the first step toward transcending them.

Transcending assumptions involves pivoting to new ways of thinking and putting in place practices that help realize shifts in thinking. This tool can be used in a number of settings: Individually with a single small group, or with several small groups. The tool acts as a task or job aid to guide the thinking process.

To use the tool, begin at the upper left corner of the page and consider the prompt within the box. Next, move horizontally across the page, pausing at each box to record your insights. Work your way left to right through each row of boxes.

Other Potential Uses of the Identifying and Transcending
Assumptions Tool

- As a prompting tool to help identify other types of assumptions.
- As a tool for identifying differences or concerns at various levels of the system (i.e., direct staff, middle management, executive leadership).
- As a tool to assist in team building or with focus groups.

Principles for Systemic Design Thinking Tool

The Principles for Systemic Design Thinking Tool was developed to provide public managers with guidelines for planning or evaluating the design of organizational systems. Checkboxes next to each principle are to be marked once a principle has been utilized in a project.

- The pre-design phase in the top row of the tool includes preparation principles.
- The design phase in the middle row includes principles to be used when designing or evaluating roles, processes, and the transfer of information and communication.
- The post-design phase in the bottom row of the tool includes principles concerning implementation and follow-up of designs.

Other Potential Uses of the Principles for Systemic Design Thinking Tool

- As a project-planning tool.
- As a review tool to show to stakeholders or funders after a project has been designed, implemented, or evaluated.

IDENTIFYING AND TRANSCENDING ASSUMPTIONS TOOL

Assumptions may take the form of generalized ideas that become untested beliefs. These untested beliefs restrict our thinking and our decisions. When designing a systemic future, identifying assumptions frees thinking, supporting greater creativity.

Instructions: Begin with a review of the left column, under "Type of Assumption," and follow the arrows across. At each stop, reflect upon and write down what thoughts or insights you have. If working in groups, share what you learned in each category.

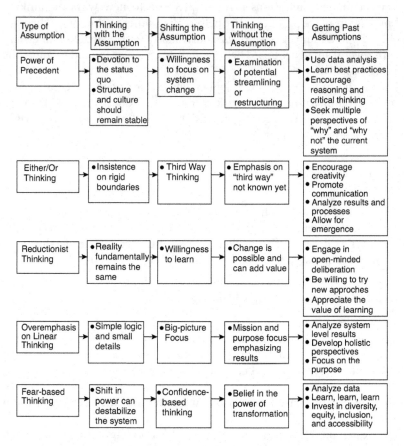

Type of Assumption	Thinking with the Assumption	Shifting the Assumption	Thinking without the Assumption	Getting Past Assumptions
Power of Precedent	• Devotion to the status quo • Structure and culture should remain stable	• Willingness to focus on system change	• Examination of potential streamlining or restructuring	• Use data analysis • Learn best practices • Encourage reasoning and critical thinking • Seek multiple perspectives of "why" and "why not" the current system
Either/Or Thinking	• Insistence on rigid boundaries	• Third Way Thinking	• Emphasis on "third way" not known yet	• Encourage creativity • Promote communication • Analyze results and processes • Allow for emergence
Reductionist Thinking	• Reality fundamentally remains the same	• Willingness to learn	• Change is possible and can add value	• Engage in open-minded deliberation • Be willing to try new approaches • Appreciate the value of learning
Overemphasis on Linear Thinking	• Simple logic and small details	• Big-picture Focus	• Mission and purpose focus emphasizing results	• Analyze system level results • Develop holistic perspectives • Focus on the purpose
Fear-based Thinking	• Shift in power can destabilize the system	• Confidence-based thinking	• Belief in the power of transformation	• Analyze data • Learn, learn, learn • Invest in diversity, equity, inclusion, and accessibility

Figure 6.2 Identifying and Transcending Assumptions Tool.

Implementation Ideas Checklist Tool

The Implementation Ideas Checklist Tool keeps track of important items to manage when implementing designs or when going through multiple design cycles. The tool can be used as an individual or group tool with which to manage implementation meetings.

PRINCIPLES FOR SYSTEMIC DESIGN THINKING TOOL

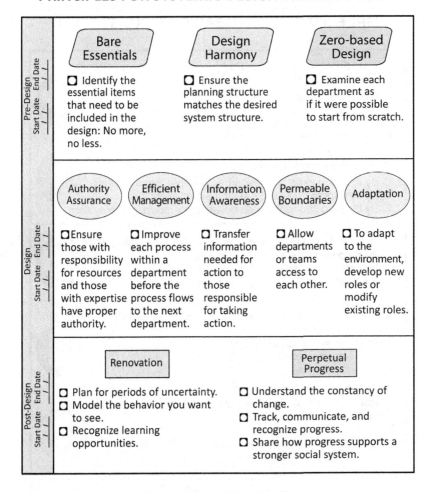

Figure 6.3 Principles for Systemic Design Thinking Tool.

Source: Adapted from Cherns (1987)

Other Potential Uses of the Implementation Ideas Checklist Tool

- As a project development tool.
- As a project management tool.
- As a tool for communicating progress to various levels of employees within the organization.

IMPLEMENTATION IDEAS CHECKLIST TOOL

1. How Might We Learn from Partners / Stakeholders / Community Members on This Project?
□ Based on function or service provided
□ Based on shared funding resources (e.g., grants)
□ Based on community needs

2. How Might This Project Build on the Strengths and Skills of Staff and Stakeholders?
□ By applying skills and resources to serve those in need
□ By developing new skills in staff and stakeholders
□ By building stronger bonds between members of the system

3. How Might We Get This Project Done in a Creative Way?
□ By recognizing who needs what and why
□ By determining the simplest way to address the need
□ By exploring how we might shorten the current process

4. How Might We Break This Project into Smaller, More Manageble Tasks?
□ To perform the action quickly
□ To ensure completion of the action
□ To assign the task to a specific individual

5. How Might We Make Sure This project Has The Greatest Impact?
□ For clients receiving our services
□ For directing resources to the people who need them
□ For making our organization stronger as a system

6. How Might We Best Communicate the Value of This Project?
□ By determining who needs to hear the message
□ By simplifying the message
□ By making the message meaningful to each audience
□ By explaining how actions will benefit each audience

Figure 6.4 Implementation Ideas Checklist Tool.

Chapter Summary

The use of design has become more common in the public sector, and the use of systemic design is gaining currency, but the idea of designing systemic futures is still in a nascent stage. When designing a systemic future, consideration should be given to the democratic values that form its foundation. Further attention should be given to time focus (e.g., future, present, past), to supporting sustainability, and to the types of design desired (e.g., organizational, service, policy). While the process of designing should be approached newly each time, there are common tasks and features that will be familiar to public managers.

The process of designing a systemic future may begin as an individual reflection—a form of planning—but quickly evolves into a group effort including the use of visuals and creative collaborations, prototyping, and experimenting. One full cycle of designing begins with listening and leads to continuous learning and improvement. Ultimately, designing a systemic future is an ongoing process of managing complexity by listening, engaging, and enacting shared ideas for change.

Practicing the Practice

Several suggestions are provided to help you expand the practice of designing a systemic future. As a public manager, your role in guiding a design mindset is important, as you bring people together and open the way toward innovative thinking. Design is about practice, and modeling openness to ideas and a willingness to try things supports the design of a systemic future.

Exploring Approaches to Designing a Systemic Future
(See Case Study)

Providing staff with an opportunity to review and discuss contrasting case studies helps staff understand what the approaches look like. The non-systemic approach will likely be more familiar to staff based on its linear and traditional approach. The systemic approach may be less familiar, but it is likely there will be some recognized elements to build upon. Your engaging staff in design thinking represents a professional development opportunity to shift their thinking toward shaping a more responsive and systemic organization.

1. Review the Non-systemic Approach in the Case Study section during a meeting and pose these questions:

    a. What were some of the benefits and drawbacks of the hospital administrator's approach to designing a systemic future?

    b. How might staff, clients, and other stakeholders react to this approach?

    c. To what extent did this approach build commitment to a common purpose?

2. Request that meeting participants read the Systemic Approach in the Case Study section, and pose the following questions:

    a. What were some of the benefits and drawbacks to the hospital administrator's approach to designing a systemic future?

    b. How might staff, clients, and other stakeholders react to this approach?

    c. What about the approach used by the administrator would benefit our own organization?

Reviewing a Current Program With Future Focus (See Figure 6.2)

Using the Identifying and Transcending Assumptions Tool, discuss a program that has been in place for several years. Engaging a group of staff and stakeholders in reviewing a current program can guide future design. Keeping the program under discussion in mind, review the tool with the group and pose the following questions:

1. What assumptions guided the design of this program?
2. To what extent are those assumptions valid now? How would you go beyond those assumptions?
3. What has worked well in this program? Provide specific examples.

    a. To what extent can those elements work well in the future?

    b. Why or why not?

4. What has not worked well in this program? Provide specific examples.
5. How should we redesign this program for the future?

Designing a New Multi-organizational Department (See Figure 6.3)

Use the Principles for Systemic Design Thinking Tool to guide the design of a new multi-organizational department. Explore the following questions to guide shared consideration of how we might approach designing a systemic future for the organization.

1. What essentials must be reflected in the design of the new department?
2. What agencies and other stakeholders need to be part of the design process?
3. How can we guide effective inter-agency collaboration during the design and implementation of the new department?
4. How can we integrate ways to communicate with all related agencies about the work of the new department?

5. How can we structure the department to ensure appropriate expertise and authority to balance and distribute resources?
6. How can we design ways for the new department to adapt responsively to a dynamic environment?
7. What have we as staff and stakeholders learned from listening to families who have experienced services related to the new department?
8. How can we build into our design a leading role in co-design and co-production for customers?

Implementing Ideas (See Figure 6.4)

Implementation involves putting a project plan into action. Use the Implementation Ideas Checklist Tool to guide the implementation of a pilot project that you and your team have designed. The questions included in the tool emphasize the strength-building of staff and stakeholders, creative thinking, impact of the project, and communicating the value of the project. Convene the project team, review the tool, ask the following questions, and take notes on people's responses:

1. How might we learn from partners/stakeholders/community members on this project?

   a. Encourage staff to brainstorm about creative ways to broaden buy-in, participation, and creativity.
   b. Use the prompts provided next to the boxes to identify specific areas of emphasis.

2. How might this project build on the strengths and skills of staff and stakeholders?

   a. Ask staff to identify ways of defining current skills and building new ones to serve in a more connected way.
   b. Use the prompts provided next to the boxes to explore ways to apply those strengths and connections with partners.

3. How can we accomplish this project in a creative way?

   a. Ask staff to discuss pathways for understanding and responding to service needs.
   b. Use the prompts provided next to the boxes to identify ways to assign and simplify tasks.

4. How might we break this project into smaller and more manageable tasks?

   a. Encourage staff to share ways to assign and shape tasks so that they are rewarding and efficient.
   b. Use the prompts provided next to the boxes to identify ways to complete tasks quickly and completely.

5. How might we make sure this project has the greatest impact?

    a. Ask staff to discuss how we can make a lasting difference for the community.

    b. Use the prompts to focus on client impact through resources and system strengths.

6. How might we best communicate the value of this project?

    a. Encourage staff to discuss how we can tell our story, so people know what we do well.

    b. Use the prompts to identify ways to determine whom to tell and ways to shape the message.

Reflecting on Practicing the Practice

Reflection on the practice of designing a systemic future encourages stepping back and looking at the bigger picture. Thinking about, writing about, and discussing the chapter, using the tools, and practicing the practice allows you to consider ways to ensure a sustained commitment and realization of a vibrant and impactful organizational system. Reflecting can take place as an individual or group activity. Consider the following questions and write or discuss your responses:

1. What worked about the practice of designing a systemic future?
2. What did not work about the practice?
3. What did you notice about your own thinking during the practice?
4. What did you notice about the interactions and behaviors of others?
5. What shifts in systemic future design occurred as a result of practicing this practice?
6. What might you do differently the next time you practice this practice?

Recommended Readings

On Creativity

Cleese, J. (2020). *Creativity: A short and cheerful guide.* Crown.

    This is a very short, easy-to-read book that makes the idea of being creative both accessible and fun for all. We chose this book because it makes creativity a less daunting and more likely prospect.

On the Genesis of Design Research in Education

Brown, A. L. (1992). Design experiments: Theoretical and methodological challenges in creating complex interventions in classroom settings. *The Journal of the Learning Sciences, 2*(2), 141–178. https://doi.org/10.1207/s15327809jls0202_2

In this article, Brown reviews her progression from a traditional educational psychologist to one engaged in the more systemic approach of design research. Although focused on education, this article was selected because of the author's articulation of issues with purely positivistic and quantitative approaches to complex problems and the benefits she found from using a design research approach.

On Managing Complexity

Lewis, M. (2021). *The premonition: A pandemic story*. W. W. Norton & Company.

In the context of the U.S. government's reaction to the pandemic, this book tells the story of several people who contributed their expertise despite meeting bureaucratic obstacles along the way. We chose this book because of the compelling storytelling about people we consider to be systemic thinkers, the portrayal of their courage of convictions, and their ability to take on one of the most complex issues in modern history.

On Policy Analysis

Bardach, E. (2012). *A practical guide for policy analysis: The eightfold path to more effective problem solving* (4th ed.). CQ Press.

This book is about more than policy analysis: It is about the importance of approaching public problems with thoughtfulness and intention. We included this book because of its approach and the author's careful attention to the importance of defining a problem.

On Thinking

Kahneman, D. (2011). *Thinking, fast and slow*. Farrar, Straus and Giroux.

Kahneman describes his research with his late colleague, Amos Tversky, on how people think. Their research revealed insights into common ways people make decisions using their intuition rather than rational thought processes. We chose this book because it helped us to become better critical thinkers.

References

Bason, C. (Ed.). (2014). *Design for policy*. Routledge.

Boardman, J., & Sauser, B. (2013). *Systemic thinking: Building maps for worlds of systems*. John Wiley & Sons.

Boland, R. J. Jr., & Collopy, F. (Eds.). (2004). *Managing as designing*. Stanford Business Books.

Borins, S. (2010). Strategic planning from Robert McNamara to gov 2.0. *Public Administration Review*, 70(s1), s220–s221. https://doi.org/10.1111/j.1540-6210.2010.02278.x

Brown, T. L. (2010). The evolution of public sector strategy. *Public Administration Review*, 70(s1), s212–s214. www.jstor.org/stable/40984127

Buchanan, R. (1992). Wicked problems in design thinking. *Design Issues*, 8(2), 5–21. https://doi.org/10.2307/1511637

Calida, B. Y., Jaradat, R. M., Abutabenjeh, S., & Keating, C. B. (2016). Governance in systems of systems: A systems-based model. *International Journal of System of Systems Engineering*, 7(4), 235–257. https://doi.org/10.1504/IJSSE.2016.080313

Carvalho, S., Asgedom, A., & Rose, P. (2022). Whose voice counts? Examining government-donor negotiations in the design of Ethiopia's large-scale education reforms for equitable learning. *Development Policy Review*, 40(5), Article e12634. https://doi.org/10.1111/dpr.12634

Checkland, P. (1999). *Systems thinking, systems practice: Includes a 30-year retrospective*. John Wiley & Sons.

Checkland, P., & Poulter, J. (2020). Soft systems methodology. In M. Reynolds & S. Holwell (Eds.), *Systems approaches to making change: A practical guide* (pp. 201–253). Springer. https://doi.org/10.1007/978-1-4471-7472-1_5

Cherns, A. (1987). Principles of sociotechnical design revisited. *Human Relations*, 40(3), 153–161. https://doi.org/10.1177/001872678704000303

Diestler, S. (2020). *Becoming a critical thinker: A user-friendly manual* (7th ed.). Pearson Education.

Easterday, M. W., Rees Lewis, D. G., & Gerber, E. M. (2018). The logic of design research. *Learning: Research and Practice*, 4(2), 131–160. https://doi.org/10.1080/23735082.2017.1286367

Gharajedaghi, J. (2011). *Systems thinking: Managing chaos and complexity: A platform for designing business architecture* (3rd ed.). Morgan Kaufmann.

Herrick, J. A. (2021). *The history and theory of rhetoric: An introduction* (7th ed.). Routledge.

IDEO.org. (2015). *The field guide to human-centered design*. www.designkit.org/resources/1.html

Kaplan, S. (2011). Strategy and PowerPoint: An inquiry into the epistemic culture and machinery of strategy making. *Organization Science*, 22(2), 320–346. www.jstor.org/stable/20868864

Kernaghan, K. (2000). The post-bureaucratic organization and public sector values. *International Review of Administrative Sciences*, 66(1), 91–104. https://doi.org/10.1177/0020852300661008

Lafontaine, A. T., & Lafontaine, C. J. (2019). A retrospective on reconciliation by design. *Healthcare Management Forum*, 32(1), 15–19. https://doi.org/10.1177/0840470418794702

McGann, M., Blomkamp, E., & Lewis, J. M. (2018). The rise of public sector innovation labs: Experiments in design thinking for policy. *Policy Sciences*, 51, 249–267. https://doi.org/10.1007/s11077-018-9315-7

McKenney, S., & Reeves, T. C. (2019). *Conducting educational design research* (2nd ed.). Routledge. https://doi.org/10.4324/9781315105642

Miettinen, R., & Virkkunen, J. (2005). Epistemic objects, artefacts and organizational change. *Organization*, 12(3), 437–456. https://doi.org/10.1177/1350508405051279

National Academies of Sciences, Engineering, and Medicine. (2000). *How people learn: Brain, mind, experience, and school* [Expanded Edition]. National Academies Press. https://doi.org/10.17226/9853

Nelson, H. G. (2007). Simply complex by design. *Performance Improvement Quarterly*, 20(2), 97–115. https://doi.org/10.1111/j.1937-8327.2007.tb00443.x

Nelson, H. G., & Stolterman, E. (2014). *The design way: Intentional change in an unpredictable world.* The MIT Press.

Nzewi, O. I., Yan, B., & Olutuase, S. (2022). An analysis of the design factors of work procedures: Implications for local government administration in South Africa. *International Review of Administrative Sciences, 88*(1), 6–25. https://doi.org/10.1177/0020852319868829

Olejniczak, K., Borkowska-Waszak, S., Domaradzka-Widla, A., & Park, Y. (2020). Policy labs: The next frontier of policy design and evaluation? *Policy & Politics, 48*(1), 89–110. https://doi.org/10.1332/030557319X15579230420108

Rittel, H. W. J., & Webber, M. M. (1973). Dilemmas in a general theory of planning. *Policy Sciences, 4*(2), 155–169. https://doi.org/10.1007/BF01405730

Schön, D. A. (1971). *Beyond the stable state.* W. W. Norton & Company.

Schön, D. A. (1983). *The reflective practitioner: How professionals think in action.* Basic Books.

Scott, N. A., Kaiser, J. L., Ngoma, T., McGlasson, K. L., Henry, E. G., Munro-Kramer, M. L., Biemba, G., Bwalya, M., Sakanga, V. R., Musonda, G., Hamer, D. H., Boyd, C. J., Bonawitz, R., Vian, T., Kruk, M. E., Fong, R. M., Chastain, P. S., Mataka, K., Mdluli, E. A., . . . Rockers, P. C. (2021). If we build it, will they come? Results of a quasi-experimental study assessing the impact of maternity waiting homes on facility-based childbirth and maternity care in Zambia. *BMJ Global Health, 6*(12), Article e006385. http://dx.doi.org/10.1136/bmjgh-2021-006385

Scott, N. A., Vian, T., Kaiser, J. L., Ngoma, T., Mataka, K., Henry, E. G., Biemba, G., Nambao, M., & Hamer, D. H. (2018). Listening to the community: Using formative research to strengthen maternity waiting homes in Zambia. *PLoS One, 13*(3), Article e0194535. https://doi.org/10.1371/journal.pone.0194535

Simon, H. A. (1996). *The sciences of the artificial* (3rd ed.). The MIT Press.

Staw, B. M., Sandelands, L. E., & Dutton J. E. (1981). Threat rigidity effects in organizational behavior: A multilevel analysis. *Administrative Science Quarterly, 26*(4), 501–524. https://doi.org/10.2307/2392337

van der Voet, J., & Lems, E. (2022). Decision-makers' generation of policy solutions amidst negative performance: Invention or rigidity? *Public Administration Review, 82*(5), 931–945. https://doi.org/10.1111/puar.13462

Vickers, G. (1983a). *The art of judgment: A study of policy making.* Harper & Row (Original work published 1965).

Vickers, G. (1983b). *Human systems are different.* Harper & Row.

Werle, F., & Seidl, D. (2015). The layered materiality of strategizing: Epistemic objects and the interplay between material artefacts in the exploration of strategic topics. *British Journal of Management, 26*(S1), S67–S89. https://doi.org/10.1111/1467-8551.12080

Wilenksy, U., & Resnick, M. (1999). Thinking in levels: A dynamic systems approach to making sense of the world. *Journal of Science Education and Technology, 8*(1), 3–19. https://doi.org/10.1023/A:1009421303064

Zhu, J. M., Rowland, R., Gunn, R., Gollust, S., & Grande, D. T. (2021). Engaging consumers in Medicaid program design: Strategies from the States. *The Milbank Quarterly, 99*(1), 99–125. https://doi.org/10.1111/1468-0009.12492

Chapter 7

Conclusion

Awareness of rapid changes in the social environment has become common knowledge. Social, political, and economic changes are rife. Likewise, the perpetual flux that represents day-to-day operations in a social system organization has frustrated, puzzled, and challenged public managers. In the 6th century BC, the philosopher Heraclitus introduced the perspective that all reality is in flux and always in the process of becoming (Osborne, 2004).

Amid this perpetuity of flux, one thing is agreed: Bureaucracy alone is inadequate to meet and address the change that is now constant in the environment. The universal recognition of change and the cumbersome, slow speed of large organizations reified into bureaucracies present a persuasive case for developing new ways of thinking. Such new thinking is called upon to formulate approaches to meeting challenges in society, communities, and organizations. Ashby's (1999) Law of Requisite Variety affirms that to be viable, a system must possess at least the amount of variety or range of choices that is present in the outer environment. Viability is an inherent principle in sustainable, systemic organizations. Bureaucracies may have been associated with stability, but the systemic reality of social systems means recognizing that contemporary organizations must gain and maintain agility and flexibility to change as conditions shift. The rigidity of bureaucracies makes them comparatively cumbersome, unable to respond quickly or effectively to dynamic circumstances and human needs.

In contrast, vibrant organizational systems have a greater capacity to remain relevant as they engage in changing themselves to meet dynamic conditions in the environment. Such organizations have the capacity to be sustainable. Education, justice, and other democratic values in a systemic context provide relevant solutions for reconfiguring organizations to meet the needs of people as we together face societal environmental change. Social systems are flexible entities capable of receiving information from the environment and translating what is heard into a more precisely configured whole whose parts combine to respond. Just as neuroplasticity has

DOI: 10.4324/9781003335153-7

been recognized as a way that the brain can grow and reorganize itself, so, too, can organizational social systems transform.

Criticism of bureaucracies must not be confused with advocating for chaos or dismantling them. Quite the contrary. Systemic thinking posits tuning in to and discovering a new and natural order. Social systems can be designed by you as a public manager with courage and conviction.

Working together, inviting multiple viewpoints to engage in dialogue that guides decision-making, you as a public manager can advance toward the goal of establishing a sustainable society that is increasingly open to changing needs. How this looks may differ from situation to situation. Rather than advocating for uniformity among social systems, we argue for developing social system organizations that address the needs of the people in the areas being served.

Systemic Thinking in Vibrant Organizations

Systemic thinking represents a vivid approach to organizational functioning. As a fusion of systems thinking, critical thinking, and design thinking, systemic thinking opens the way to recognizing the connective tissue among parts of the organizational system. Systems thinking focuses on the fulfillment of the organization's purpose(s). Systems thinking differs from linear-analytical mental processing by emphasizing bringing together diverse viewpoints to reflect the wholeness of the system. Diverse viewpoints support the identification of the system in its broadest, most accurate sense. Purpose-driven action that builds upon productive connections and relationships among people, departments, organizations, and the environment constitutes systems thinking. Such an approach fortifies the system as a reliable, sustainable entity that can produce value for the people it serves.

In systemic organizations, critical thinking examines assumptions associated with organizational structure, such as policies, procedures, funding streams, and their deployment. Critical thinking is directed toward vetting assumptions by questioning the rhetoric of an organization's foundational structure. Engaging in critical thinking highlights the point that assumptions and rhetoric associated with an organization's structure are socially constructed, not absolutes.

Of great importance is the realization that organizational systems must be analyzed for their effectiveness in meeting the needs of the service population. While this may translate to efficiency, even more important is the effectiveness of service design and delivery. Critical thinking leads naturally to creative thinking, performance thinking, and idea generation, building upon divergent thinking toward convergent thinking. You as a public manager have a role to play in inviting people to ask and answer the questions, "Why not?" and "How effective can our service be?" regarding potential solutions.

Design thinking draws from systems thinking and critical thinking by blending analytical and holistic thinking to recognize how a given approach to service might be transformed. By building upon the critical thinking question: What assumptions led to the current structure? Design thinking asks: To what extent might that construct be changed to meet wholly new circumstances? Design thinking invites reflection on the usefulness of a given structure and set of processes and inspires taking action in response to client needs.

Ultimately, systemic thinking supports the depth and richness of public service by paying attention to the extant layers of meaning and context in interactions with everyone involved in public management. In recent decades, public organizations have been encouraged to perform "more like business," meaning to emphasize efficiencies wherever they can be realized. While such efficiencies can be beneficial, they must be supplanted by effectiveness that considers the systemic reality of public social systems.

Mandated to engage and serve the public, government, nonprofit, and nongovernmental service is admittedly more complex than private sector work (Collins, 2005). Public service necessitates the inclusion of many different entities in shaping how services are funded, delivered, and assessed. One of the major benefits of systemic thinking in social systems is that it affords the ability to balance requisite regulation with the pressures of desirable innovation. Achieving such a feat is well within the reach of vibrant organizations.

The Five Practices in Vibrant Organizations

The five practices for creating a vibrant organization are mutually reinforcing. Not only does each practice add specific value, but each also supports and leads to the use of other practices. The complement of the five practices stimulates new learning about the system as it currently exists and reveals how the system might be transformed to meet continually emerging needs and opportunities for service. The interdependence of the five practices is depicted in Figure 7.1.

For example, depicting the system is an inclusive practice that involves dialogue and specification of how the system is currently configured. Identifying, defining, and visualizing the system generates a clear picture of the social system as understood by staff, stakeholders, and clients. The range of viewpoints contributed during successive iterations of the practice of depicting the system supports increasing accuracy in the rendering of the system picture. Once the system is depicted to the satisfaction of the participants, issues associated with evaluating the system emerge. One focal question is, "How well does the system work for those who depend on it for delivering services?"

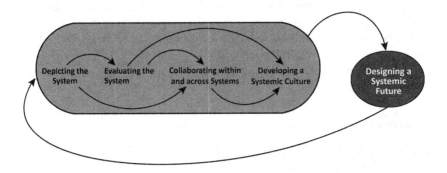

Figure 7.1 The Five Practices in Vibrant Organizations.

The practice of depicting the system further leads to the practice of collaborating within and across systems. Given the system picture generated while engaging in the practice of depicting the system, another question arises, "Who else needs to be actively participating in the system?" Participation in collaborative activity potentially transforms the system while adding value to considerations associated with culture. Culture-building is a conscious process that adds range and depth of perspective and enriches the capacity of the system.

Democratic values characterize a systemic culture. Finding ways to express democratic values such as equality and justice, to listen for their expression, and to resolve the inevitable conflicts that arise due to their expression is part of the process of developing a systemic culture in public organizations. Communicating about the systemic nature of the organization and developing employees' understanding of systemic thinking and learning are important elements of building a systemic culture.

The fourfold composite of practices, including depicting the system, evaluating the system, collaborating within and across systems, and developing a systemic culture, leads to designing a systemic future. In turn, this future design leads back to these processes and continually guides the integration of a new reality that reflects the discovery of a renewed system. Within this smooth, evolutionary process, organizational transformation is poised to occur.

While enhancing the capacity of the social system, the ongoing engagement of staff and stakeholders in the five practices for creating a vibrant organization stimulates and recreates a sense of bonding and bridging social connection that establishes the system as a flexible and thoughtful entity capable of changing the environment it serves. Far from a passive, rote approach to participating in an organization, the five practices enacted iteratively provide a way of making the best use of a diverse array of talent that bespeaks the reality of a social system designed to serve responsibly and flexibly.

A vibrant organization is easily recognizable. It is characterized by ardent, proactive communication and a commitment to learning. Such learning requires patience, compassion, and an appreciation of employees' experience and expertise.

Practice With Tools and Systemic Integrity

In a vibrant organization, you as a public manager bring the five practices to life by developing fluency in applying their associated tools. You author your own systemic thinking through the frequent and ongoing application of tools that have been researched and refined with public sector managers and instructional designers. A major benefit of tools application to support the five practices is that it provides benefits that transcend the often touted high-performing organization by achieving systemic integrity.

In place of a competitive construct, systemic integrity is focused on the organization's reason for being in the public sphere. Each facet of practice, whether defining the system, evaluating, collaborating, developing a systemic culture, or designing a systemic future, benefits from the application of relevant individual tools that add clarity and depth to systemic thinking at all levels of the organization. Systemic integrity is enlivening for stakeholders of the system as it provides a palpable sense of wholeness and purpose at the center of shared commitment to public service. Vibrant organizations are humanizing environments characterized by focused attention to listening and alertness to the needs and perspectives of people whose lives are intertwined with our own.

Day-to-day benefits of tools application and systemic integrity include the realization of clear, tangible service, practical learning, and discovery. For example, the Identifying and Transcending Assumptions Tool (Figure 6.2) guides groups of people in developing a needed skill that offers an opportunity to bond through learning and application. Likewise, the Systemic Knowledge Wheel Tool (Figure 5.5) guides you as a public manager in the use of performance information relevant to the organizational system. You shape your approach to balancing focal points of emphasis based on the use of the tool. In each case, the tools are structured to secure insights and put observations and ideas to work on behalf of the system.

Additional benefits of tools application include establishing a means of sharing and developing skills among employees, leading to pride in participation and performance. A vibrant organization is characterized by a genuine sense of belonging, in which each person embraces his or her role and consciously connects responsibilities to those of others within the department and with those departments providing complementary services.

Broader benefits of continuous practice and establishing systemic integrity include an integrated sense of the functions of a system identified by Beer (1972). These functions position the organization to review and improve performance using the Formative Feedback Loops Tool (Figure 3.2) and the Systems Analysis Tool (Figure 3.3). These systemic evaluation tools facilitate awareness of effective service and performance across the organization.

Community benefits can be recognized by the Social Capital Mapping Tool (Figure 4.3), which shapes the conscious design of outreach and community building around the purposes of the organizational system. Reasons for and ways of building social capital mean infusing connectivity, power, and authority into the system. This tool generates awareness while providing a vehicle for planning system effectiveness for the communities served.

The Empathic Reality of Vibrant Organizations

Vibrant organizations reflect a view of human history as evolving toward fundamental and essential empathy, in stark contrast to the long-held view that the nature of human beings was self-interested, aggressive, and primarily invested in individual survival. Rifkin (2009) shaped an integrated history of the empathic reality of the human species. Such empathy has characterized the growth and development of human consciousness toward an evolved higher state.

The very premise of this book is that systemic thinking and vibrant organizational systems depend on human connectivity and clarity of purpose in service. You as a public manager face the challenge of shaping your organization to address significant challenges in the world. While human systems have become challenging to maintain (Vickers, 1983), there exists a systemic imperative to engage with the soft systems approach that is appropriate for meeting the complexity faced in today's world (Checkland, 1999; Checkland & Poulter, 2020). Ultimately, you as a public manager can have a profound impact on the social systems that exist to serve people empathically in a connected world.

References

Ashby, W. R. (1999). *An Introduction to cybernetics*. Chapman & Hall. http://pcp. vub.ac.be/books/IntroCyb.pdf (Original work published 1957).
Beer, S. (1972). *The brain of the firm*. John Wiley & Sons.
Checkland, P. (1999). *Systems thinking, systems practice: Includes a 30-year retrospective*. John Wiley & Sons.
Checkland, P., & Poulter, J. (2020). Soft systems methodology. In M. Reynolds & S. Holwell (Eds.), *Systems approaches to making change: A practical guide* (pp. 201–253). Springer. https://doi.org/10.1007/978-1-4471-7472-1_5

Collins, J. (2005). *Good to great and the social sectors: A monograph to accompany good to great.* Harper Business.

Osborne, C. (2004). *Presocratic philosophy: A very short introduction.* Oxford University Press.

Rifkin, J. (2009). *The empathic civilization: The race to global consciousness in a world in Crisis.* Jeremy P. Tarcher/Penguin.

Vickers, G. (1983). *Human systems are different.* Harper & Row.

Index

Note: Page numbers in *italics* indicate a figure and page numbers in **bold** indicate a table on the corresponding page.

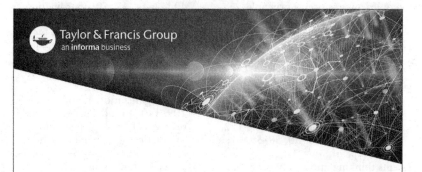

Printed in the United States
by Baker & Taylor Publisher Services